Memory, Place and Identity

Memory, Place and Identity

The Cultural Landscapes of Cornwall

edited by Garry Tregidga

First published by Francis Boutle Publishers
272 Alexandra Park Road
London N22 7BG
Tel/Fax: (020) 8889 7744
Email: info@francisboutle.co.uk
www.francisboutle.co.uk

ISBN 978 1 903427 73 6

Contents

List of illustrations

Introduction

Garry Tregidga

Cornwall has been explored in many books and articles in recent decades. Studies range from archaeological accounts of the area's prehistoric past to the contemporary concerns of the New Cornish Social Science; from local histories of Cornish communities to the Great Emigration of the nineteenth century.[1] Central to many of these investigations has been the notion that Cornwall's distinctive sense of place ensures that it is 'different' from other parts of the United Kingdom. Even in 1933 the Civil War historian Mary Coate could write that the 'history of Cornwall is that of a county with a strong personality, priding itself on its peculiarities and alive with a local patriotism rooted in racial differences and fed by geographical isolation'.[2] By the 1990s such views had become central to the research agenda of the University of Exeter's Institute of Cornish Studies. Philip Payton writing in *The Making of Modern Cornwall* concluded that 'in each historical period the experience of Cornwall has been highly individual when compared to that of the English "centre", or indeed other areas of Britain'.[3] The aim of this book is to explore the iconic importance of landscape in shaping this sense of difference. In contrast to a conventional historical focus on a particular period or subject it considers specific places that make up Cornwall both to highlight the various ways in which the region has been constructed and to capture the sense of spatial diversity that exists alongside expressions of unity. A particular emphasis is given to the significance of cultural memory. Pierre Nora's concept of 'Les lieux de Mémoire' or 'sites of memory' has surprisingly not been applied in any great detail to the Cornish experience.[4] By considering the cultural remembrance of place from an inter-disciplinary perspective this collection of essays offers new perspectives on the cultural construction of Cornwall.

The inherent importance of the spatial dimension to Cornish Studies has been recognised in recent decades. An early example was Trevor Burston's photographic perspective on St Michael's Mount in 1995. Burston highlighted the importance of 'national symbols such as Big Ben, the Eiffel Tower, the Statue of Liberty [as] visual clichés on an international scale'.[5] The Mount was similar since its visual impact on the

St Michael's Mount in West Cornwall (photograph courtesy of Three S Films)

landscape of West Cornwall, combined with its photographic reproduction via postcards, publications and souvenirs, meant that it had emerged as an 'icon' for Cornwall itself. Like Mount Fuji in Japan, it symbolised a land of legend, romance and pilgrimage.[6] This was followed two years later by a pioneering collection of essays edited by Ella Westland on the cultural construction of 'Cornwall'. The emphasis was placed firmly on the different ways in which the region has been imagined, with Westland commenting that 'the landscapes we are now trying to understand are made in our minds'.[7] Contrasting representations of Cornwall were investigated with chapters on such subjects as Virginia Woolf's depiction of St Ives, storytelling in the Clay Country and Thomas Hardy's relationship with North Cornwall.[8] By the end of the decade historians were also starting to discuss the construction of place in a Cornish context. This was particularly the case in the Cornish History Network with individuals like John Probert, Ronald Perry and Sharron Schwartz raising the issue of differences between local communities, thereby challenging the earlier Cornucentric assumptions of New Cornish Studies. It was claimed that 'In some senses there is no such thing as Cornwall as it includes such a diversity of regions' and that there was a 'need for finer-mesh, Intra-Cornwall studies'.[9] Building on this debate Bernard Deacon proposed a new agenda in 2000 for the study of place when he stressed the importance of the so-called 'spatial turn'. He concluded that space was 'fundamental to the Cornish Studies project' with the researcher needing to 'stay alert to processes that operate at different scales: the global, the Cornish and the local'.[10]

But the actual processes and meanings associated with Cornwall's sense of place still require detailed study. Despite occasional articles with a specific connection to the 'spatial turn', there has surprisingly been no serious attempt to bring together ongoing work in this area.[11] That research needs to be conducted on an inter-disciplinary basis since it was noticeable that many of the micro investigations included in Westland's *Cultural Construction of Place* came from a purely literary perspective. Moreover, the growing interest in the importance of cultural remembrance provides a useful framework for understanding the power of place in a Cornish setting. Studies in the 1990s ranging from Nora's *Realms of Memory* to Simon Schama's *Landscape and Memory* have opened up new possibilities.[12] This approach has been applied in recent years to some of the other Celtic nations. A good example is Guy Beiner's research into the long-term impact of the French invasion of Ireland. Even in the mid-twentieth century stories and songs passed down over several generations were still shaping cultural and political narratives in the Irish countryside.[13] The Celtic Diasporas have also started to be covered with Celeste Ray and others highlighting the importance of memory and place in sustaining the transatlantic connections between Scotland and Scottish Heritage movements throughout North America.[14]

These developments provide the context for understanding *Memory, Place and Identity*. The book brings together a team of scholars drawn from a variety of disciplines including archaeology, history, literature and media studies to explore the power of place. Building on the ongoing work of the Cornish Story programme at the Institute of Cornish Studies the volume looks at the transmission of cultural memory through such mediums as oral tradition, festivals, monuments, written texts and physical landscapes. A creative synergy between the written word and photography is also established in order to gain greater insight into the psychological power of place. As Anna Tonkin explains, 'It is perhaps too tempting to reiterate the age-old cliché "a picture is worth a thousand words", however it is not coincidental that from the early days both amateur and professional photographers have followed a strong desire to capture and share the image of place'. She adds that a 'photograph becomes a visual gateway to a memory of place, even to those furthest in distance, and in the case of a landscape no longer in existence. The old engine house, the deserted beach, the open cliff top; these images become synonymous with Cornwall's strong cultural memory of place'.[15] *Memory, Place and Identity* seeks to develop the field of both Cornish and Celtic Studies by engaging with wider trends in both community-based research and cultural memory studies. By opening up new avenues of research it is possible to gain a greater insight into the impact of the past upon the present. Key questions relating to place and landscape are posed. How does the past relate to the present? Why are particular places remembered through time? What is the role of landscape in the construction of Cornish identity?

The opening chapter explores the prehistoric world of West Cornwall. Mel Giles and Laura Cripps show how the cliff castles of the area constructed their own sense of place in the landscape. Significantly, archaeological investigations into such sites reveal the presence of earlier traces of previous societies. A sense of continuity through time was created so that cliff castles came to have a particular importance as community locales in subsequent periods. Alan Kent moves the discussion forward in time and place through a chapter that examines the relationship between language, literature and landscape. This contribution to the debate is based on his investigations into the neglected Arthurian traditions of mid-Cornwall and the language and festival culture of Mousehole. Kent suggests that both sites of memory provide useful insight into the renegotiation of Cornish ethnicity through time with contrasting ideological perspectives shaping our construction of specific places. This focus on multiple interpretations of the past is a reminder of Robert Gildea's 'contention that there is no single ... collective memory but parallel and competing collective memories, and that the past is constructed not as fact but as myth, to serve the interest of a particular community'.[16]

The politics of cultural memory features prominently in the subsequent chapter. Words like 'independence', 'rebellion' and 'defiance' feature prominently in popular discourses relating to Cornish culture. It is suggested that the conflicts of the Early Modern period, notably the provincial rebellions of the Tudor period and the Civil War of the 1640s, created a cultural memory of communal resistance that still reinforces the language of popular protest in contemporary Cornwall. Underlying this connection between past and present is a spatial network of sites stretching from West to North Cornwall. Plaques and statues provide permanent memorials to that rebellious past in places like St Ives and St Keverne. But such cultural markers require the actions of individuals and groups in society. David Thomson points out that in Truro in the early nineteenth century there was often a reluctance to commemorate the achievements of local citizens. Even the prominent Lander statue emerged by accident rather than as part of a conscious attempt to encourage civic pride. Thomson speculates that this reflected class divisions with civic leaders from the 'upper' middle class more interested in metropolitan London than the local agenda of Truro's 'shopocracy'. Yet remembrance is not a static process since it reflects changing circumstances. Truro is a good example since from the second half of the nineteenth century onwards its status was further enhanced by the building of a new cathedral and separate diocesan status. Cornwall's cathedral, which was intended as 'a place of hallowed memories' dating back to the 'Brito-Celtic Church of West Wales', became the focus of a new process of memorialization.[17] With city status in 1877 Truro was certainly an obvious place to commemorate the wider territorial identity of Cornwall. This was a point made by Tim Shaw, the artist responsible for the controversial Drummer statue installed outside Truro's Hall for Cornwall in 2011:

> It's an honour to have been commissioned to create a major artwork for Cornwall's city centre. When I first set foot in Cornwall 25 years ago, I described it as a place whose drumbeat drums differently to anywhere else. This sculpture aims to define Cornwall and its people, who have a quiet and proud sense of independence matched with an instinct to survive whatever the prevailing circumstances might be.[18]

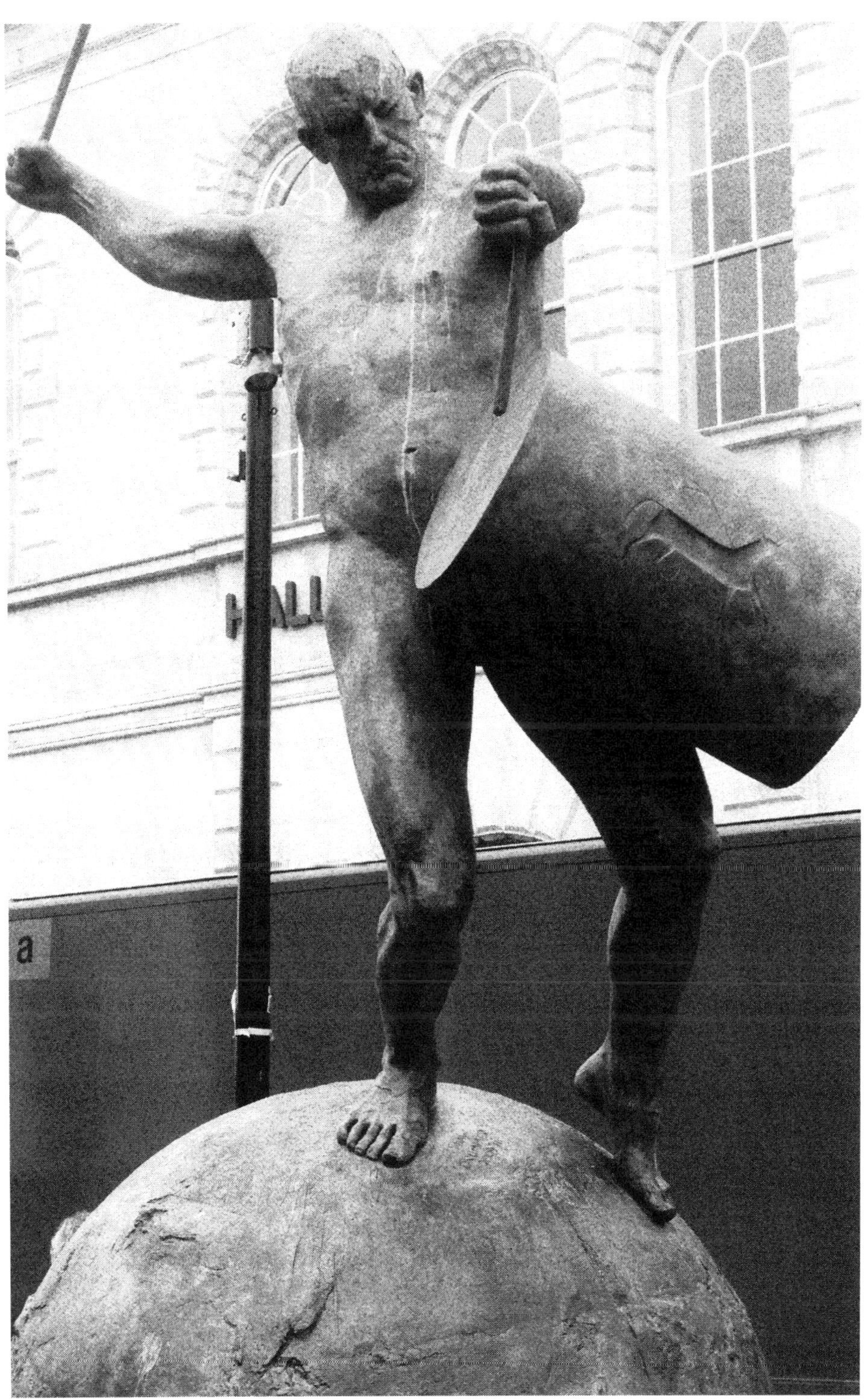

Drummer statue in Truro (Photograph by Anna Tonkin)

Shaw went on to use the words 'ancient', 'timelessness' and 'magic' to describe the Cornish landscape that inspired the Drummer. Such comments reflect the often mystical quality associated with the power of place.[19] The spiritual landscape of Cornwall itself has been constructed and contested at many different levels with interpretations ranging from its traditional image as the 'Land of the Saints' to an otherworldly Celtic space for contemporary pagans: from the chapel landscape of Cornish Methodism to the surfing rituals of coastal tourism. Recent memory studies have focused on the distinctive culture of Cornish Methodism, which emerged as the dominant religious force west of the Tamar and accounted for over 60% of religious worshippers in 1851.[20] But in this particular study consideration is given to Cornish Anglicanism. Graham Busby focuses on the three churches of Gunwalloe, Lanteglos-by-Fowey and St Just-in-Roseland to suggest that religious heritage can play an active role in the articulation of 'Cornishness'. He argues that increasing globalisation and mobility has led to greater choice in the lives of individuals, concurrently leading to a search for personal identity. This includes visitors from overseas in search of their genealogical roots in Cornwall. Drawing on content analysis of comments in church visitors' books, the past is shown to influence the personal construction of identities. This emphasis on the narratives of self is continued by Monica Emerich. In her chapter based on a research visit to Cornwall she takes an auto-ethnographic approach to the ways in which perspectives in the American Healthy Living and New Age media contest, mirror and support discourses about spiritualised geographies in Cornwall. Conventional Celtic landscapes, such as standing stones, dolmens and holy wells, are contrasted with the representations of others whose everyday experiences, religious beliefs and cultural memories are tied to an alternative set of places and meanings.

Occupational identities can also draw on specific sites of memory. Schwartz's 2008 study of the personalities and stories associated with Cornwall's mining landscape is a good example. Using oral history recordings from the Cornish Audio Visual Archive (CAVA) she highlighted the often complex notions of identity connected to this once dominant industry.[21] But here the focus shifts to another industrial landscape. Jesse Harasta focuses on the competing discourses associated with the visitor centres of the Eden Project and the Wheal Martyn China Clay Country Park in mid-Cornwall. In his view the ideological struggle for supremacy in the Clay Country raises wider considerations over the cultural and ethnic construction of Cornwall itself. Farming and fishing can also be regarded as symbolic occupations in Cornwall. Robert Keys investigates the folklore of the Rame peninsula in South-East Cornwall with a particular focus on the fishing community of Portwrinkle and its agricultural hinterland. After discussing the decline of fishing and the transformation of the area by the arrival of tourism and retirement homes the chapter considers some specific examples of stories passed down through oral tradition. Keys concludes that rural folklore continues to be replenished which suggests that it still provides a useful purpose in contemporary society.

The theme of occupational identity is continued by Kay Milden who puts the horticultural industry of the Tamar Valley under the spotlight. Oral history interviews are used to capture the sense of change that took place in recent decades. Many of the wooded valley slopes were transformed into a patchwork of small market gardens, and then consequently reverted back to woodland after the demise of the industry. Milden also places herself within the narrative of 'full circle' through her family connections with the Tamar Valley, thereby highlighting issues relating to the role of the indigenous researcher in memory and landscape studies. The final chapter by Geoff Swallow considers the myths of surfing and coastal tourism. In recent decades surfing has become an icon of a new Cornwall that by its very nature challenges older cultural representations associated with its mining past. Swallow focuses on the Cribbar, regarded as Cornwall's biggest and best known wave, to show how the oral narratives of pioneer surfers provide an important source of myth in identity formation in a coastal resort like Newquay. In that sense the Cribbar can be regarded as a deeply symbolic site that links past and present. It is also a useful reminder of the way in which the nexus of memory and place continues to shape the ongoing story of Cornwall.

Notes

1. Examples include Caradoc Peters, *The Archaeology of Cornwall: The Foundation of our Society*, Cornwall Editions Limited, 2005; Malcolm Williams, 'The New Cornish Social Science' in Philip Payton (ed.), *Cornish Studies: Ten*, University of Exeter Press, 2002, pp. 44-66; Sharron Schwartz and Roger Parker, *Lanner: A Cornish Mining Parish*, Halsgrove, 1998; Philip Payton, *The Cornish Overseas: A History of Cornwall's Great Emigration*, Cornwall Editions, 2005.
2. Mary Coate, *Cornwall in the Great Civil War and Interregnum*, 1642-1660, Clarendon Press 1933, p. 1.
3. Philip Payton, *The Making of Modern Cornwall: Historical Experience and the Persistence of Difference*, Dyllansow, Truran, 1992, p. 2.
4. Pierre Nora (ed.), *Realms of Memory: The Construction of the French Past*, Columbia University Press, 1996.
5. Trevor Burston, *The Floating World: 36 Views of St Michael's Mount*, Royal Institution of Cornwall, 1995, p. 3.
6. Ibid, pp. 3-10.
7. Ella Westland (ed.), *Cornwall The Cultural Construction of Place*, Patten Press, 1997, p. 1.
8. *Ibid*.
9. John Probert, 'Are Cornish Studies going in the wrong direction?, *Cornish History Network Newsletter*, Issue 4, March 1999; Sharron Schwartz, 'Migration to the USA c1815-1930: Preliminary Comparative Demographics for Redruth and St Austell Registration Districts, *Cornish History Network Newsletter*, Issue 6, November 1999; Ron Perry, 'State Uniformity, Regional Unity and Local Diversity in Cornwall, 1870-1914, *Cornish History Network Newsletter*, Issue 6, November 1999.
10. Bernard Deacon, 'In Search of the Missing "Turn": The Spatial Dimension and Cornish Studies' in Philip Payton (ed.), *Cornish Studies: Eight*, University of Exeter Press, 2000, pp. 213-30.
11. Kay Milden, 'Are you Church or Chapel? Perceptions of Spatial and Spiritual Identity within Cornish Methodism' in Philip Payton (ed.), *Cornish Studies: Twelve*, University of Exeter Press, 2004, pp. 144-165. Garry Tregidga, 'Electoral Landscapes: The Political Ecology of the Clay Country since 1885' in Philip Payton (ed.), *Cornish Studies: Seventeen*, University of Exeter Press, 2009, pp. 117-35.
12. Simon Schama, *Landscape and Memory*, Harper Collins Publishers, 1995.
13. G. Beiner, *Remembering the Year of the French: Irish Folk History and Social Memory*, University of Wisconsin Press, 2006; G. Beiner, 'The Mystery of the Cannon Chains: Remembrance in the Irish Countryside' in *History Workshop Journal*, 66, 2008. See also Edward Cowan and Richard Finlay (eds.), *Scottish History: The Power of the Past*, Edinburgh University Press, 2002 and J.Githens-Mazer, *Myths and Memories of the Easter Rising: Cultural and Political Nationalism in Ireland*, Irish Academic Press, 2006.
14. Celeste Ray (ed.), *Transatlantic Scots*, University of Alabama Press, 2005.
15. Email communication with Anna Tonkin, 18 March 2012. The publication brings together photographs by Sarah Chapman, Ted Giffords, Robert Keys and Anna Tonkin along with illustrations from the postcard collection of Mac Waters.
16. Robert Gildea, *The Past in French History*, Yale University Press, 1994
17. Rev W.S. Lach-Szyrma, *A Church History of Cornwall and of the Diocese of Truro*, Netherton and Worth, Truro, 1889.
18. See http://www.thisiscornwall.co.uk/Artist-talk-long-awaited-Truro-sculpture/story-11520879-detail/story.html, 14 April 2011 (last accessed 18 March 2012).
19. http://www.bbc.co.uk/news/uk-england-devon-13873729 (last accessed 18 March 2012)
20. Milden, 'Are you Church or Chapel?' in Payton (ed.), *Cornish Studies: Twelve*, 2004, p. 149.
21. Sharron P. Schwartz, *Voices of the Cornish Mining Landscape*, Cornwall County Council, 2008.

Cliff castles and the Cornish landscape

M. C. Giles and L. J. Cripps

Its situation to describe,
It seems a Castle by Sea side,
With ancient Walls environ'd round,
The Castle with this Rock is Crown'd

Poem from 1815; the cliff castle described is Treryn Dinas, the 'rock', Logan rock.

The cliff castles of the Cornish coastline have drawn generations of people to the very edges of the earth. They occupy some of the most prominent headlands on the south western peninsula and have become landmarks enshrined in legend and folklore. Castle Treen, mentioned in the above poem, is widely known as a home of giants, spriggans (Cornish elves), and at least one ghost.[1] For sites so prominent within popular culture however, cliff castles remain some of the most elusive and intriguing monuments in the archaeological record.

In previous analyses, cliff castles (or promontory forts as they are also known), have been interpreted primarily upon the basis of their defensive capabilities and coastal location, both of which are seen as enhancing their potential as trading centres.[2] The overwhelming conclusion continues to be that cliff castles, in their social context and function, are the same as Iron Age hillforts but simply 'on the coast'.[3] Certain cliff castles have been identified alongside specific hillforts as playing a central role in Early/Middle Iron Age social organisation; in West Penwith for example, Maen Castle, Bosigran and Trencrom have been suggested as elite centres, charged with the administration and control of scarce or shared resources; 'one of the key functions of the higher levels of relatively unsophisticated rural societies'.[4]

This traditional, hillfort-centric model of Iron Age societies has been the subject of much critique in recent years.[5] More significantly for the discussion here however, this traditional consensus appears to be governing the interpretation of cliff castles as landscape monuments, whilst helping to maintain the presumption of an 'unsophisticated' regional Iron Age society. Many cliff castles do employ impressive banks and ditches as part of their enclosure and several show evidence for structures, and in some cases extensive occupation. However, these sites are best characterised by their inherent variation in structures and features, indicating substantial differences in function, use and meaning. In addition, a narrative dominated by the defensive capabilities and trading potential of cliff castles has largely overlooked their more curious and special aspects; their engagement with other landscape features, both natural and man made, and their proximity to the sea. It is, after all, the unusual and often dramatic nature of these headlands, their vistas and their ambiguous situation between both land and sea, that provides a sense of awe and wonderment to visitors today, and it should not be surprising if this was an aspect of their construction and meaning in the past. The remote locations of many cliff castles has lead to a more recent recognition of a possible communal religious function,[6] but the rationale behind this, or evidence for this, has yet to be proposed.

Visitors at Trencom (Photograph by Anna Tonkin)

This paper does not aim to offer any detailed appraisal or deconstruction of the traditional views of cliff castle form and function, but instead will concentrate upon alternative ways to view their use and meaning. These were sites in which Iron Age communities negotiated their own sense of place in the landscape, and explored their relationships with both local and more distant communities. They were also spaces in which traces of the past, in terms of earlier prehistoric features and human remains, made a more ancient presence 'present' in the world with them, constructing a deeply rooted sense of history and belonging. It was through this richly layered series of encounters that the cliff castles came to have a particular importance as community locales, in the lives of later prehistoric groups within the region.

Ramparts to unite and divide

Only four cliff castles in Cornwall have been subject to recorded excavation (The Rumps, Trevelgue Head, Gurnards Head and Penhale) and these have notably targeted rampart areas over interiors. This is the result of an overt interest in sequence, date and military potential, over the character of inhabitation at these sites, and changes over the long-term. As a result, details of the so-called 'defensive capabilities' of cliff castles tend to dominate more general discussions, particularly within popular field guides and local history books.[7] Let us begin, therefore, with the issue of their defensive features.

The presence of ramparts and ditches can be seen as consolidating – and even exaggerating – the defensive capability of the site. The majority of cliff castles in Cornwall employ multiple banks and ditches, which are frequently massive; the inner and middle ramparts at The Rumps for example were approximately 25ft wide/9ft high and 32ft wide/12ft high respectively.[8] Importantly, these powerful barriers divorce already isolated promontories from the landmass beyond. They reflect the commitment of hours of sweat and labour in their construction, as well as the attendant social support that made such programmes of work possible. We do not know whether these were built periodically, involving the aggregation of small groups every year, over a long period of time, or in one more sustained campaign. However, by embodying communal labour, and possibly orchestrated power, they became impressive monuments of the community in their own right. The degree to which they might have formed a real physical barrier to the movement of both people and animals, varies substantially, depending in part on their situation and architectural elaboration. Many of the more ephemeral features evidenced by post or stakeholes, have yet to be uncovered.

However, it is overly simplistic to explain the cliff castles of the Cornish coast in purely defensive terms. At the Rumps, hut circles, gullies and domestic material were found outside or between ramparts, as well as in the interior. This does not exclude the defensive capabilities of the enclosure circuit, but it would appear to suggest that the 'occupation' at some sites was less prescribed than is traditionally suggested. In addition, certain cliff castle ramparts would be notably difficult to 'defend'. At Treryn Dinas for example, the innermost rampart that separates the rocky promontory of Castle Treen from the rest of the headland, is directly overlooked. It might be argued that this makes the site more vulnerable to attack, yet this aspect has been noted at a number of hillfort sites.[9] The rampart at Treryn Dinas might therefore be regarded as more of a conceptual barrier, separating one very distinct area from another.

All 'barriers' (ramparts, ditches, walls and banks) are social as well as physical; they define, divide and distinguish. They describe what is 'inside' as separate and different from what is 'outside', and can therefore be used to circumscribe particular groups, or make evident a transition in time, space or state of social being.[10] Different rules or

The Boulders of Trencrom (Photograph by Anna Tonkin)

codes of behaviour may therefore be expected inside these spaces, and thresholds between the interior and exterior are often seen as highly charged: potentially dangerous and liminal. However, we have yet to investigate promontory forts with these ideas in mind.

Two out of the three cliff castles to experience the partial excavation of their ramparts displayed an increase in the number and monumentality of their ramparts over time, these being The Rumps, excavated in the 1960s[11] and Trevelgue Head, excavated in 1939.[12] On this basis it would seem likely that the ramparts of several other cliff castles may have become more numerous and elaborate with time; particularly those perhaps that exhibit different forms of rampart construction (e.g. Treryn Dinas, Chynhalls Point, Giants Castle). Again, this could be interpreted as part of an intensified 'militarization' of the site. However, the process of constructing and maintaining banks and cutting and re-cutting ditches would have been time consuming, and would have required considerable labour, particularly when the size and depths of the ditches are considered, several of which were rock cut. More recent excavations of Iron Age enclosures elsewhere in Britain have been able to identify phases of ditch re-cutting and in several instances this appears to have occurred in distinct sections, indicating perhaps, that a number of small groups or households joined to take part in the maintenance of communal enclosures. Whatever the scale of labour involved, the process of maintaining and elaborating cliff castle ramparts would have engaged individuals within a joint activity that helped constitute the physical bounds of a community, beyond the local kin group. As such, the construction, maintenance and reformation of these ramparts would have provided an opportunity to reiterate social ties and reinforce a sense of communal identity.[13] In the course of such work, opportunities arose for new aspects of identity or forms of authority to emerge. By *attending* to place then, people were also attending to the bonds which sustained their broader social and political life.

These may have included trade and exchange with more distant communities, although the evidence for this is scant. As Cunliffe has noted,[14] the sea is not always seen as a boundary; in prehistory in particular, it was a medium of communication, giving rise to an Atlantic 'seaboard' of social networks and contacts. Exotic pottery, decorated bronze fittings and blue glass beads have been found at a variety of sites (e.g. Gurnards Head, Trevelgue Head) and the discovery of large numbers of stones of a similar size from sites such as Penhale have been interpreted as weights for trading transactions, although they may equally have been gathered for sling-shot. The cliff castles certainly provided excellent sea vistas, which would have been useful for monitoring sea-traffic, or providing settings in which to perform rites for ensuring safe passage over water. They would have also provided dramatic settings in which to receive guests or strangers, including potentially hostile encounters. In particular, their role and significance in the later Iron Age-early Roman period, has probably been underestimated.

Reclaiming the past

The process of re-excavating ditches and consolidating ramparts would also have involved re-discovering material such as pottery and flints from both the recent and distant past, providing a palpable sense of history and the longevity of landscape use, which in turn would have caused individuals or groups to situate themselves within a broader social context, past and present. As will be argued below, there can be no doubt that the communities of the later prehistoric period would have been acutely aware of the built fabric and artefactual material that they often, perhaps unintentionally, encountered and 'like archaeologists ... would have been forced to use these ancient scraps of material culture to understand their place in the world'.[15] Making a direct association to or with a feature of the landscape, or object from antiquity was thus one way in which later prehistoric communities could have interacted with their past. This not only involved traces of human activity at such sites but the rock outcrops, crags and shoreline sculpted by the forces of sea and wind. Later prehistoric communities may have made no distinction between ancient human and elemental features: both would have demanded an explanation of how they came to be this way, and what their relationship was with the groups who inhabited these places. They would have been named and known, associated with particular histories, literally 'soaked' in meaning. This, along with oral tradition, is one way in which the cultural memory of a group can be maintained, reproduced and/or transformed, and can be used to link directly to notions of cultural identity, cultural history and to a sense of longevity and legitimacy of place.[16]

With this in mind, a slightly different perspective might be brought to bear on aspects of the construction and maintenance of cliff castle ramparts, their position within the landscape, and their relationship to other landscape remnants. At Maen Castle for example, an earlier Bronze Age lynchet from a network of field systems that expanded across the headland, was incorporated into the Iron Age rampart of the cliff castle. This caused the rampart to kick out, and deviate from its original course. Although the incorporation of an earlier field boundary within the ramparts of the new enclosure could be seen as a logical, labour-saving initiative, the incorporation of this feature into the physical boundary of the cliff castle enabled a direct association to be made between the enclosure and the previous inhabitants who used the headland. A sense of this time depth would have been easily retained through the visible kink of the boundary. Through the recognition and association with past activity upon the headland, be it of known family members or appropriated ancestors, the community of the cliff castle may have reiterated their legitimacy, as well as their longevity and sense of place, both to the outside world and to themselves.

This type of approach may help to explain the location and situation of several other cliff castles in Cornwall. Many coastal locations that were transformed into cliff castles during the Iron Age also appear to have had significance in the Bronze Age. At Kenidjack Castle for example, a hoard of 30 pieces of tin and copper and two unsocketted axes were found just outside of the enclosure ramparts. It suggests people were coming to these sites for generations, to hide things, make offerings or negotiate with supernatural forces. However, the majority of visible Bronze Age activity around coastal headlands appears to be more specifically related to death, and therefore ancestry. Two Bronze Age bowl barrows are situated within the ramparts at Treryn Dinas cliff castle, and another two within the interior of Trevelgue Head. Half a mile up the coast from Trevelgue a further two Bronze Age bowl barrows are prominent, close to the cliff edge. Two more Bronze Age barrows were enclosed within the interior of Dodman Castle. In addition to the barrows at Treryn Dinas, sherds of a Bronze Age cremation urn have been found, alongside pottery of Iron Age date, eroding from paths within the interior. Certain coastal promontories clearly had special mortuary significance for the Bronze Age communities of Cornwall, making them appropriate places to communicate with forebears. Long-term cultural memory of these 'special' places and their ancient monuments may have influenced their enclosure during the Iron Age, and the deliberate association of new features with traces of a more ancient, perhaps even mythical past.[17] In this way, communal memories were constructed through new monuments which referenced the past, reinforcing a strong sense of community identity, legitimacy and belonging, and perpetuating a particular world-view.[18]

In this light, it is interesting to note that although cremation seems to have been the dominant mortuary tradition in Cornwall during the Iron Age, we lack substantial evidence for firmly dated graves or cairns inland. As dramatic, liminal spaces, poised between the world of the land and the world of the sea, it is possible that cliff castles played an important role in these rites: water is often seen as a medium through which the deceased depart into their next life.[19] However, we have yet to explore cliff castles for evidence of funerary pyres, or investigate the idea of scattering remains into the sea.

Isolation and liminality

It has been argued that the significance of specific coastal locales to both Iron Age and Bronze Age communities can actually be traced to their interest in features from much earlier periods, especially the late Neolithic-early Bronze Age. Even where there are no obvious monuments, it has been suggested that the very act of enclosure is mimicking much earlier traditions. Sharpe has suggested that the enclosure of particularly rocky headlands during the Iron Age (e.g. Maen Castle, Treryn Dinas, Gurnard Head) may have been an attempt to mimic the granite enclosures further inland, such as Carn Brea and Trencrom, which are known to be, or are likely to be, Neolithic in date.[20] These sites also witness a resumption of settlement activity in the Iron Age; Carn Brea has known structures of Iron Age date,[21] and pottery from the second century BC has been collected from molehills at Trencrom.

If the rocky nature of headlands was a factor in their choice for enclosure, then it is apparent that the position of ramparts and entrance ways at certain sites was much more visually and experientially strategic than is traditionally acknowledged. They orchestrate the passage of entry, frequently controlling the approaching view of the coast-line to dramatic effect. This is most clearly seen at Treryn Dinas where the height and position of the outer ramparts allow for only the very top of Castle Treen, the outer most promontory, to be observed upon approach. Because of the contrast between this very rocky promontory, and the more rounded headland before it, Castle Treen would have appeared to be an island, divorced from the land, as people approached. The entrances of the two outermost ramparts further constrain movement through the narrow middle rampart, channeling people into the interior along a course that maintains this visual illusion.

It is the harsh, rocky and jagged topography of most cliff castle headlands, the noise and scent of the sea, the wind buffeting up over the promontory, and the strangely sheltered calm in the lee of the ramparts, which are central to the creation of a sense of isolation at these sites. As noted before, the ramparts and ditches of the cliff castles, and occasional towering rock outcrops, further divorce already isolated promontories from the mainland. They frame and accentuate this division, creating peripheral, liminal spaces: conceptual 'islands' surrounded by the sea, with infinite vistas to the horizon. This feeling of being within another world is accentuated by the cacophony of seabirds, nesting, feeding and wheeling through the air. To be within such sites frequently involves a giddy sense of disorientation and sensual submersion in the sounds, smells and forces of the meeting point between land and sea: a state of mind in which experiences of key rites of passage or transitional life-events may have been particularly dramatic. Equally, they would have provided an impressive setting for encounters and negotiations with people from over the waters, or from distant regions further inland.

Such settings provided locales in which to be seen (dramatically skylined from land and sea) but also to see. It was from such vantage points that coastal visitors would have been seen, allowing those inland to prepare for their arrival. It was a place from which to watch dramatic storms and the flotsam and jetsam they brought, and perhaps negotiate with whatever forces were thought to inhabit the waters. Finally, from such clifftops, people could observe and judge the passage of marine life like seabirds, shoals

A view from Trencrom (Photograph by Anna Tonkin)

of fish, or rarer creatures rising from its depths.

Cliff castles also defined spaces in which potentially dangerous activities could occur. Social encounters and exchanges have been discussed above, but at Trevelgue Head for example, there is substantial evidence for metalworking. Although tin and iron ore can be found nearby, and the promontory forts provided strong sea breezes to drive the furnace or smelt, there may be other reasons why this craft was carried out in the setting of the promontory fort, as ironworking in particular is frequently associated with physical and spiritual danger.[22] During the Iron Age, the skill to create weapons, tools and ornaments from fuel and ore, may have led to its association with creative and transformative power. As a result, on other Iron Age sites, it is often carried out in isolated enclosures, away from normal 'domestic' settlement:[23] cliff castles may have provided an appropriate alternative, in this landscape setting.

There are some examples of cliff castles that do not appear to employ distinctive promontories in this way (e.g. Round Wood, Kelsey Head). But none of these have been excavated and in several instances features within their interior imply a different period of use and/or specific purpose.

Conclusion

It has not been the intention of this paper to provide a thorough deconstruction of the various roles and functions suggested for cliff castles, nor to offer a detailed breakdown of the excavated evidence form these sites. Rather, we have tried to highlight a conceptual 'sea-change' which we believe could profitably alter the way in which we think about, perceive and interpret the meanings of these sites in the Iron Age. Not all cliff castles have such dramatic settings on promontories and some seem to have associated with what we might regard as 'normal' domestic occupation and inhabitation. Yet others are distinctively different, with varied and unique histories. We have suggested that their proximity to the coast, their frequently dramatic use of space and orchestration of movement, and the very special sense of liminality created between land and sea, would have coloured and influenced every event and activity which took place on these promontories. Coupled with a sense of the ancient past, they were actively used to negotiate the relationship between people and place, and between local and more distant groups, including those perhaps, of the ancestors. We prefer then, to think of them less as defensive forts or castles, than '*theatres of the sea*'.

Notes

1. *Prehistoric Society Summer Conference: June 1996*, Cornwall Archaeological Society, 1996.
2. For examples see B. W. Cunliffe, *Iron Age Communities of Britain*, Routledge, 1991, pp. 257-59; P. Herring, 'The Cliff Castles and Hillforts of West Penwith in Light of Recent Work at Maen Castle and Treryn Dinas' *Cornish Archaeology*, 33, 1994, pp. 40-56; N. Johnson and P. Rose, 'Defended Settlement in Cornwall: An Illustrated Discussion' in D. Miles (ed.) *The Romano-British Countryside: Studies in Rural Settlement and Economy*, BAR British Series 103, 1982, pp. 151-208; R. G. Lamb, *Iron Age Promontory Forts in the Northern Isles*, BAR British Series 79, 1980; H. Quinnell, 'Cornwall during the Iron Age and Roman Period', *Cornish Archaeology*, 25, 1986, pp. 111-134.
3. Johnson and Rose, 'Defended Settlement in Cornwall', 1982, p. 155 . See also M. Todd, *The South West to AD 1000*, Longman, 1987, p. 163.
4. Herring, 'The Cliff Castles and Hillforts of West Penwith', *Cornish Archaeology*, 33, 1994, p. 45.
5. J. D. Hill, 'Hill-forts and the Iron Age of Wessex' in J. Collis and T. Champion (eds.), *The Iron Age in Britain and Ireland: Recent Trends*, Sheffield Academic Press, 1996, pp. 95-116. J. Stopford, 'Danebury: An Alternative View', *Scottish*

Archaeological Review, 14, 1987, pp. 70-75.
6. B. W. Cunliffe, *Facing the Ocean*, Oxford University Press, 2001, p. 364.
7. Todd, *The South West*, 1987, pp. 163-5. C. Weatherhill, *Cornovia*, Cornwall Books, 2000.
8. R. Brooks, 'The Excavation of the Rumps Cliff Castle, St Minver, Cornwall', *Cornish Archaeology*, 13, 1974, pp. 5-50.
9. M. Bowden and D. McOmish, 'The Required Barrier', *Scottish Archaeological Review*, 4, 1987, pp. 76-84. M. Bowden and D. McOmish, 'Little Boxes: more about Hillforts', *Scottish Archaeological Review*, 6, 1989, pp. 12-16.
10. R. Hingley, 'The Archaeology of Settlement and the Social Significance of Space', *Scottish Archaeological Review*, 3, 1, 1984, pp. 22-27.
11. Brooks, 'The Excavation of the Rumps Cliff Castle, St Minver, Cornwall', *Cornish Archaeology*, 13, 1974.
12. J. Nowakowski, *Trevelgue Head, Cornwall. Appraisal of 1939 Excavations and Design for Assessment*, Cornwall Archaeological Unit Report, 2000.
13. See M. Giles, 'Refiguring rights in the Early Iron Age landscapes of East Yorkshire' in C. Haselgrove and R. Pope (eds.), *The Earlier Iron Age in Britain and the near Continent*, Oxbow, 2007, pp. 103-118; N. Sharples, 'Building communities and creating identities in the first millennium BC' in C. Haselgrove and R. Pope, (eds.), *The Earlier Iron Age in Britain and the near Continent*, Oxbow, 2007, pp. 174-84; A. Wigley, 'Rooted to the spot: the 'smaller enclosures' of the later first millennium BC in the central Welsh Marches' in C. Haselgrove and T. Moore (ed.), *The Later Iron Age in Britain and Beyond*, Oxbow, 2007, pp. 173-189.
14. Cunliffe, *Facing the Ocean*, 2001, p. 9.
15. R. Bradley, *The Past in Prehistoric Societies*, Routledge, 2002, pp. 13-14.
16. Ibid. See also J. Brück and M. Goodman, *Making Places in the Prehistoric World*, UCL Press, 1999; C. Gosden and G. Lock, 'Prehistoric Histories' World Archaeology, 30, 1998, pp. 2-12; C. Gosden and Y. Marshal, 'The Cultural Biography of Objects', *World Archaeology*, 31, 1999, pp. 169-178.
17. J. Barrett, 'The Mythical Landscapes of the British Iron Age' in W. Ashmore and A.B. Knapp (eds.), *Archaeologies of Landscape*, Blackwells, 1999, pp. 253-68.
18. Bradley, *The Past in Prehistoric Societies*, 2002.
19. See B. Bevan, 'Land–Life–Regeneration: Interpreting a Middle Iron Age Landscape in Eastern Yorkshire' in B. Bevan (ed.), *Northern Exposure: Interpretative Devolution and the Iron Age of the British Isles*, Leicester University Press, 1999, pp. 123-148. J. Downes, 'Cremation: a Spectacle and a Journey' in J. Downes and T Pollard (eds.), *The Loved Body's Corruption*, Cruithne Press, 1999, pp. 19-29.
20. A. Sharpe, 'Treryn Dinas: Cliff Castles Reconsidered', *Cornish Archaeology*, 31, 1992, pp. 31-38.
21. R. Mercer, A. Legge, J. Samuels, I. Smith and A. Saville, 'Excavations at Carn Brea, Illogan, Cornwall – a Neolithic Fortified Complex of the Third Millennium BC', *Cornish Archaeology*, 20, 1981, pp.1-204.
22. E. W. Herbert, *Iron, Gender and Power*, Indiana University Press, 1993.
23. R. Hingley, 'Iron, Iron Working and Regeneration: a Study of the Symbolic Meaning of Metalworking in Iron Age Britain' in A. Gwilt and C. C. Haselgrove (eds.), *Reconstructing Iron Age Societies*, Oxbow, pp. 9-18. M. Giles, 'Making metal and forging relations: ironworking in the British Iron Age', *Oxford Journal of Archaeology*, 26, 4, 2007, pp. 395-413.

From Igraine ingrained to callin' 'ome Mouzel: Two paradigms of memory, language and literature in Cornwall

Alan M. Kent

Introduction: Cultural Place-Making in Kernow

This chapter seeks to deconstruct and demystify two locations and landscapes seemingly 'ingrained' in the imagination and collective memory of the indigenous Cornish population, as well as visitors to the territory. In so doing, it seeks to renegotiate cultural and critical memory in these populations, and demonstrate how, in fact, over time, aspects of the Cornish Revival and tourism agencies and authorities have been complicit in the creation of an 'imagined' past which might at best be at arms length to, or at worse distant from the historical truth. Such a critical re-evaluation comes in the light of two trends in scholarship over the past two decades. Firstly, this is a response to the transformations in cultural geographic theory, where debates over the ideology of culture and the production of 'value' and 'memory' have facilitated a new interface between critical and geographical ways of seeing.[1] This so-called 'cultural turn' in the fusion of cultural studies and geography has brought about a new emphasis upon the complexities of place, and a sometimes specific focus on territories where identities, processes and landscapes are contested. Clearly, given Cornwall's unique geo-political and geo-linguistic position (where Anglo-Cornish, Cornu-English and Cornish are collectively in operation at any one point),[2] it is certainly a suitable case for treatment within this new cultural place-making.

The second trend in academia may be traced back to the work of observers such as Simon Schama, who in his influential 2004 text *Landscape and Memory*, has re-examined the impact landscape has had on our culture and imaginations.[3] Schama suggests that place and the power of memory are in fact, much more pervasive in cultural thought than was previously realised. Landscape, once only the defined realm of archaeologists,

Viewing the landscape from St Dennis church (Photograph by Anna Tonkin)

geologists and geographers was now the concern of literary scholars, cultural historians and socio-linguists. New connections between space and place were being made – driven by cultural determinants. At the same time, other texts have re-defined anthropological investigations into historical change and memory, noting the connections between place, space, identity and nationalism in varied and different settings across the world.[4] In turn, the focus on the memory of communities has led to a reinvigorated engagement with what was known in the past as 'Oral History'. Given the new trends in cultural place-making and in memory-driven anthropology, then it was perhaps obvious that the field of 'Oral History' would be drawn into concerns over place, writing and identity.[5] Displacement and dispossession could now be examined in the light of locality, with the field having far more of an interdisciplinary focus. The twin concerns of this volume (Memory and Place) are therefore part of a broader reappraisal, not just concerned with what I have previously termed 'an unresolved duality of place' in Cornwall,[6] but of moves in cultural studies elsewhere, in both the European and global context.[7]

Such readings have undoubtedly influenced a range of work emerging in the Cornish context that has responded to these transitions. The field of literary studies within Cornish Studies has increasingly had to deal with the above issues of place, space, identity and memory.[8] Work by Symons, and Goodman, for example, has located the cultural geographic significance of the work of the Anglo-Cornish novelist and poet Jack Clemo.[9] Such work is important because it alters the perceived memory of Clemo – instead of him being a marginal figure in British literary studies, it locates his work in the 'Centre' and reappraises his texts along the lines of memory and place. Payton, and Brace, for example, have considered the affect of landscape in the writings of the Anglo-Cornish poets John Betjeman and Arthur Caddick respectively.[10] Lavan and Murdoch too, have considered these issues amongst the more challenging field of Cornish Medieval literature.[11] Such responses are important in helping to understand the longer term linkages between memory and landscape dating from the Medieval literature, even though Payton has been forced to admit that in general, New Cornish Studies had 'failed to draw on historians of the Medieval period'.[12] Related to this critical energy on memory and landscape has, of course, been new conceptualisations and understandings of the geo-political make-up of the United Kingdom, particularly in the moves towards devolution in Wales, Scotland and Northern Ireland since 1997.[13] Given Cornwall's own distinctive cultural 'memory' or longing for devolution, there is a necessity for literature, landscape and memory to be read with this agenda in mind.[14]

This said though, there are still texts emerging which purport to look at 'sense of place' related to Cornwall but which almost universally fail to do so, because the observers have not critically re-examined the canonical literature, emergent or re-discovered literature, landscape or its impact upon collective memory.[15] Such works have either followed a line of enquiry which is outmoded, or have stuck to a broadly uncompromising medievalist perspective, which has not bothered to engage with contemporary critical perspectives which suit Cornwall's geo-political and geo-linguistic state.[16] Given, for example, the observations made below on Arthuriana, such a reluctance to work outside of the comfort zone of Medievalism, one shares Payton's frustrations. It is worth noting that it is important to respond to these new and emerging trends within literary and cultural studies because otherwise it is hard for Cornish Studies (being a relatively small and emergent discipline) to hold its own within academia.[17]

This chapter will examine two aspects of the interface between landscape, language and literature. The first focus will be upon Arthuriana within Cornwall. I have chosen this focus because Arthuriana is seemingly one of the most monolithic and unmoveable aspects of Cornish cultural geography. Not only are its values, sites and ideologies ingrained in the imagination and memory of the Cornish, they are also uniquely bound up with wider British and European agendas of space and place.[18] Cultural memory therefore proves hardest to shift with Arthuriana. The second interface is the location of Mousehole,[19] which in Cornu-English parlance is particularly interesting to 'call home' (a phrase meaning 'to remember') since not only is it a 'draw' to those concerned with the Cornish language, but it also finds its own cultural memory and geography manipulated within contemporary Cornwall's seemingly unstoppable heritage and festival culture. These twin foci will inform our debate over memory and place.

Never mind Tintagel, here's Castle-an-Dinas

Within the collective memory of Cornwall, one touchstone into the mythic past and its landscapes is offered by Arthuriana. King Arthur has many associations with Cornwall, not least, for example, that the Chough, the 'national' bird of Cornwall, is said to represent the spirit of King Arthur.[20] The modern Cornish Gorsedd ceremony (established in 1928) has similar Arthurian matter at its core. In Part 13 of the proceedings, the Deputy Grand Bard declares:

An als whath Arthur's wyth,
Yn corf Palores yn few:
Y Wlas whath Arthur a bew;
Myghtern a ve hag a vyth!

[Still Arthur watches our shore,
In guise of a Chough there flown:
His Kingdom he keeps his own,
One King, to be King once more.][21]

This declaration is responded to by all of the bards present with the words '*Nyns yu marow Myghtern Arthur!* [King Arthur is not dead!]' followed by a collective touch (each bard's hand placed on the shoulder of the one before them) of a ceremonial sword representing Excalibur. These public assertions are matched by a wider interest in this material (and the sister corpus of Tristana),[22] as well as on-going scholarship from a number of different fields investigating aspects of this collective memory of landscape and place.[23] As Kent, Hale and Saunders have documented, Cornwall and its geography form the source of much of the Arthurian corpus, and although transmogrified and altered through the centuries through different political and cultural agendas, nevertheless the tourism and heritage industries have retained an interest (or perhaps even an obsession) with this body of material.[24]

There has over the centuries, however, been a transition of the memorial landscape of Arthur, from perhaps how it was signified to the Cornish and how it has been represented to the wider world. In fact, it is very clear that for the Cornish version of events, other landscapes have key significance when compared to the major centre of 'public' Arthuriana in Cornwall at Tintagel. It is perhaps not surprising though that Tintagel has come to represent *de facto* Arthuriana. Many layers of experience, literature, folklore and archaeology have contributed to this association, and then there is the landscape at Tintagel itself – a spectacular island – linked to the mainland by a tiny constriction (almost constructing in the imagination the perfect fortress).[25] The literary-historical connection between King Arthur and Tintagel was completed relatively early on, by Geoffrey of Monmouth in 1136.[26] Indeed, the 'perfect fortress' concept may have been the model of locale that Geoffrey was seeking. Geoffrey claimed that his 'History' was based on an ancient British book (discussed by some scholars as perhaps being in Old Cornish).[27] His telling was in fact, a compendium of historical and mythological material imaginatively blended into a continuous narrative, which displayed the glory of the Britons. Charles Thomas has neatly shown how the 'mythos' of Arthur has been nurtured and grown at Tintagel over the centuries.[28] Historical texts, along with the establishment of modern institutions such as King Arthur's Great Hall of Chivalry in the early 1930s, have embedded the importance of Tintagel in both modern Cornish consciousness and that of the wider world.[29]

Tintagel's placing in the geography of Arthur has in reality, however, been accentuated out of all proportion. Digging under the surface of how memory in Cornwall traditionally dealt with the Arthurian matter, we find that other landscapes actually had greater significance. In two rarely considered articles written in 1912 and 1927, Henry Jenner (1893-1934) examined issues of memory and place relating to Arthuriana in Cornwall.[30] In his 1912 article, Jenner was at pains to explore the wider geography of Arthuriana in Cornwall, beyond mid and north Cornwall. He was perhaps seeking to show that there were connections elsewhere, though rightly comes to cautious conclusions about their significance and etymology. What is interesting about the article is that it is one of the first modern evaluations of this material from a distinctly Cornish point of view. Several landscapes and locations are considered; among them Bosigran, Bosworlas, Botallack, Merlin's Rock, Vellandruchar and Rosemodress. Some of these are worth exploring in slightly more detail. Bosigran could recall the name of Arthur's mother – Igraine; *Bos* meaning 'dwelling-place'. However, Jenner himself realised that the name could be connected with the Cornish *egr* [a daisy]. A recent translation of the place-names by Weatherhill suggests 'dwelling at Chycarn [lost name]'.[31] Thus although Igraine may be desirable in order to open up the Arthurian geography, it can hardly be said to be 'ingrained' in landscape and memory, as we shall see below in the way that places such as Castle-an-Dinas and Demeliock are. Jenner's logic follows a similar application on Bosworlas, which he offers might mean 'dwelling of Gorlois'. Whilst this might desirable, close as it is to Bosigran, the etymology cannot be guaranteed. The difficulty is that while some locations are demonstrated by Jenner as convincingly having links, modern place-names studies would be far more cautious in

attesting a link.[32] Igraine and wider Arthuriana may therefore not be so 'ingrained' in West Penwith as in mid or north Cornwall.

Jenner's second paper of 1927 in essence is a follow up of the research completed in 1912. Drawing on his manuscript knowledge, Jenner was broadly dismissive of the significance of Tintagel in the Arthurian corpus of Cornwall. In his view, Tintagel's place was founded on dubious associations, and that its rise in the 1920s and 1930s in particular, as a tourist destination failed to celebrate what he regarded as the 'authentic' cultural memory of Cornwall – embodied in the Cornish language and its literature. Importantly, as we shall see below, Jenner also argues for the importance of both Demeliock and Castle-an-Dinas. Indeed, it is his contestation that Geoffrey's source book would have mentioned Demeliock and that it also probably mentioned the 'Dinas' – which Jenner argues Geoffrey transformed into Tintagel (what he terms *Oppidum*) rather than the more likely Castle-an-Dinas site. Jenner also pointedly argues that Geoffrey actually only mentions Tintagel once in the whole of his text.[33]

The earlier Cornish historian William Hals (1655-c.1737) also offers useful insight on the cultural memory of King Arthur. In his vast and ambitious (and still unpublished) history, *The Complete History of Cornwall* (c.1736) Hals devotes a section of his text to what he terms 'The History of King Arthur and his Progenitors'.[34] Hals' initial focus in his narrative is on the collective deeds of Uther Pendragon and to this extent he explains how Uther lays 'siege to the Castle of Demeliock'. Demeliock is managed by Gorlois, and Hals notes that this is a 'trebble wall'd fortification of earth' (suggesting

Postcard of Tintagel from the early 1900s (Mac Waters postcard collection)

a hill fort). Making no breakthrough and realising that Igraine is housed at Dundagell (Tintagel) Uther is given advice to seek out the 'British Prophet' Merlin in order to help conceal himself to Igraine. Igraine's place and function in the narrative is therefore extremely important. Not only is she native Cornish and married to Gorlois, but she is also Arthur's mother. Hals again 'ingrains' her into the narrative at this point. She is both a Mary-figure and temptress. When the narrative shifts onto Arthur it is the Romans who he must defeat, alongside a final battle with Mordred. In Hals' account this final battle take place at Camelford and that after he has received his mortal wounds Arthur is taken to 'the vale of Avallan (i.e. the Apple Valley) near Glastonbury'.

Certainly here we have an interesting depiction of the importance of the landscape at the location of Demeliock. Modern-day Demellick Manor lies some quarter of a mile from the hillfort of St Dennis (the church sits in the centre of the fortifications).[35] Thus conflation of the two locations is possible, as indeed is the name Dennis itself. Although it may well refer to the Saint Denis of Francis (one of the Seven Champions of Christendom) it is possible that it is a mutation of the Cornish *Dinas* [Hillfort or Castle].[36] This would be the preferred locale for Gorlois's residence under attack from Uther. If so, then it would stand to reason that some two miles directly to the north, the location of Castle-an-Dinas might have been the base for Uther's army.[37] Given Hals' version of events, there is certainly a memory of Arthurian material in this location, whether the two sites are separate places, or actually conflated into one.

This view of the landscape in mid-Cornwall is supported by the extant Cornish-language literature. The c.1504 text *Bewnans Meriasek* [The Life of St Meriasek], a play focused on the narrative of a Breton saint who establishes a church at Camborne – features an Arthur-like 'Duke of Cornwall' who is one of the few figures who stands up to the tyrant Teudar.[38] In one of his speeches, the Duke of Cornwall expresses an understanding of his cultural geography. In performance, this clearly draws on a memorial understanding of the extent of the dukedom, as well as expressing the significance of the location of Castle-an-Dinas. By this time, it seems Tintagel was already shifting into the consciousness of the audience as being the 'chief dwelling seat' but nonetheless, the drama still asserts the importance of the mid-Cornwall location:

Me yv duk in oll kernow
indella ytho ov thays
hag vhel arluth in pov
a tamer the pen van vlays
tregys off lemen heb wov
berth in castel an dynas
sur in peddre
ha war an tyreth vhel
thym yma castel arel
a veth gelwys tyndagyel
henna yv ofen tregse.

[I am Duke in all Cornwall:
So was my father,
And a high lord in the country
From Tamar to the Land's End.
I am dwelling now, without a lie,
Within the castle of Dynas
Surely in Pidar,
And in the high land
I have another castle,
Which is called Tyntagel:
That is my chief dwelling seat.][39]

Payton has usefully read the play, and in particular, the figure of Teudar as an allegory of post-1497 Cornwall.[40] This reading might suggest residual memory of locations such as Castle-an-Dinas and Tintagel as icons of Cornish resistance to occupation and accommodation. The memorial associations of these landscapes have been expressed on numerous occasions by both organisations and individuals, countering what is seen as cultural imperialism. In this sense, we have seen the leading paradigms of cultural geographic studies at work: those of dispossession and displacement. With regard to Arthurian matter, this is usually seen as being English Heritage, who control and manage many of the significant sites.[41]

Bewnans Ke [The Life of St Kea] – written around 1500 but surviving in an incomplete manuscript from the second half of the sixteenth century – provides additional insight on this memory of Arthur which has almost disappeared.[42] If we go with Hals' account of the Arthurian matter, then clearly the play echoes the established conflict between Arthur and Mordred. In the narrative, Arthur leaves his nephew Mordred in charge, says goodbye to Guinevere and departs for France to meet the Roman Lucius. The two armies battle, and Arthur defeats and kills Lucius, sending his severed head back to Rome. Meanwhile, Mordred and Guinevere conspire to usurp the throne, and Mordred is crowned king. Arthur hears of this treachery and assembles his counselors, while Mordred allies with the Saxon Cheldric. Arthur returns to Britain, and the two armies clash. This is the moment that Hals also details in his account. The play text breaks off during a scene with Guinevere in the castle (presumably one of the hill forts), while the end is missing. If it followed the *Life*, Kea would have re-entered the picture. In the *Life*, Kea is summoned to mediate between Arthur and Mordred, but he comes to realise that the endeavor is futile. He cannot alter the destiny of the 'matter of Britain'. Kea heads back to Brittany, stopping in Winchester where he castigates Guinevere. The remorseful queen enters a convent.

Kea returns to Cléder, where he eventually dies peacefully. The geography of the final battle between Arthur and Mordred is not specified in the drama, nor the *Life*, but there is one extant place-name which might indicate a possible link back to the mid-Cornwall landscape close to Demeliock and Castle-an-Dinas. Intriguingly, this is Tremodrett Farm [Modrett's Farm] near Roche.[43] Sadly the link is perhaps too tenuous to make any further assertion about Mordred's presence in this part of Cornwall. It is a

piece of 'desired' memory connecting the narrative to the landscape perhaps, but one we must remain sceptical of.

Regardless of this, the importance of *Bewnans Ke* in terms of re-thinking cultural memory is threefold. First of all, although scholars had often considered there might exist a Cornish text with Arthurian material,[44] since its discovery in 2000, this play formally identified a link between such matter and the geography of Cornwall. Secondly, the play confirmed that a core aspect of the Arthurian matter for the Cornish was the betrayal of Arthur by Guinevere and Mordred, and that this somehow culminated in a final battle – ending the achievement of Arthur's reign and setting the 'tragic' destiny of the matter of Britain. Thirdly, although the conflict with the Romans might seem historically inaccurate (the Saxons are usually posited in the Cornish mindset as the enemy), the text holds them up as 'imperialist and cultural other' (like the Saxons) who are encroaching on the matter of Britain.[45]

The parish church of St Dennis (Photograph by Anna Tonkin)

There is one final twist to this aspect of cultural memory in mid-Cornwall. In Hals' history he acknowledges that one of his sources was a now lost text called the *Book of the*

Acts of King Arthur. He credits the authorship of this work to John Trevisa (c.1342-1402).[46] Trevisa is perhaps best known as one of the greatest Middle English prose translators of Latin texts into English, but he was also perhaps initially educated at the Collegiate Church of Glasney College in Penryn.[47] Curiously enough, Trevisa was born not far from the location of Castle-an-Dinas and present-day St Dennis, at St Enoder. This may well have been natural material for Trevisa to apply himself to, knowing the landscape intimately. There may even, of course, be a connection between his *Book of the Acts of King Arthur* and the way the dramatist/s behind *Bewnans Ke*, conceived of the matter.[48] There are certainly enough similarities between Hals' narrative and the material of the play to suggest a possible common genesis. Certainly what this shows is that for pre-modern cultural memory, it seems that although Tintagel was known of, that single location did not represent for the Cornish the key landscape in the Arthurian corpus. Such a covert and overt manipulation of symbol, text and landscape is therefore highly visible within the Arthurian matter in Cornwall. We shall now consider another aspect of memory and manipulation in relation to the geography of Mousehole.

Mouzel, Memory and Manipulation

There could be a number of communities and landscapes above and beyond those related to Arthuriana which I might have addressed in this chapter in which memory and invention create cultural place-making. Some which readily come to mind are the way, for example, the landscape of Fowey and its surrounds (as inspiration, lifestyle and romance) are imagined as part of the Daphne du Maurier Festival.[49] There is also the way in which the South Crofty area of Pool is now reconfigured as the Heartlands Project, despite a cult and populist literature which tells a different narrative about the authentic collective memory of that community.[50] Both are narratives in which seemingly the authorities wish to 'ingrain' a certain cultural memory and yet both are locales in which that narrative of space and place are problematical. The Daphne du Maurier Festival is perceived as part-celebration of Cornwall's cultural and literary identity and yet it is one that is seemingly only really defined by Britain-wide 'stars' and 'turns' who the authorities can bring to Cornwall.[51] The Heartlands project faces different challenges of fusing past identity and memory with a Cornish economy and community fit for purpose in the twenty-first century. In 2012, this balance between past and present was neatly achieved by Miracle Theatre and English Touring Opera's production of *Tin* (based on the 1888 novel by Edward Bosenketh).[52] In this way, past cultural memory of tin-mining is celebrated in the new surrounds of a progressive venue. Similar balances of progression and dispossession are almost a constant issue in twenty-first-century Cornwall.

One community which strikes this observer as being of interest in this way is the village and landscape of Mousehole. The significance of Mousehole [Cornish: *Porthinnis*] as epicentre of the decline of the Cornish language fits the hegemonic cultural memory of Cornwall for both the indigenous population and visitors alike. Mousehole is a fishing community in West Cornwall. Memory dictates that perhaps Cornish would have lasted longer here because the language's decline is generally seen by the Cornish Revival as being in an East-West direction,[53] and because the assumed folklore is that

fishermen and women would have retained the language longer because of the isolation and organic simplicity of their work. Mousehole's geographical position in West Penwith has enhanced this memory: it is a community conveniently close to Newlyn and Penzance, but at the time separate from them. For the visitor, it therefore offers achievable 'Celtic detachment' without too much cultural adjustment; the latter a wider metaphor perhaps, for memory and place are sought by visitors to Cornwall.

Much celebrated in the village (and in close by Paul) is the life and 'legend' of Dolly Pentreath (1692-1777), the so-called last native speaker of Cornish. Mousehole itself is an important centre for the memory of the Cornish language. For example, John Keigwin (1642-1716), the well-known scholar and translator of the *Ordinalia* and *Pascon Agan Arluth*, was a resident. Other prominent figures include Oliver Pender, William Gwavas, and William Bodinar. There is not the space here to outline all the work completed by individuals writing in Late Cornish, but a number of observers offer accounts. Dolly Pentreath herself was enshrined in legend when she was visited by the antiquarian Daines Barrington in 1768, who later presented a paper on her to the Society of Antiquities in 1773.[54] Much folklore and misinformation about Dolly's life has built up over the centuries, although the centenary of her death is now regarded by several observers as the ignition point of the modern revival of the Cornish language.[55] Over the years however, the symbol of Dolly Pentreath as the 'last speaker' has been manipulated by the tourist industry. It is seen as being fitting since Mousehole is both the antithesis of modernity and is perceived as being 'very' Cornish. Therefore it is apt that the 'last speaker' is to be found here. In present-day Mousehole, not only is Dolly Pentreath's house marked by a plaque (a suggested destination in many travel guides

Postcard depicting Dolly Pentreath at Mousehole

over the years)[56] but her image and iconic stance forms the background to numerous souvenirs and postcards.

We know from recent scholarship on the retreat of the Cornish language, that although the East-West decline is very much the general trend, there were also pockets of resistance occurring in certain areas. Often, these areas were not necessarily fishing villages but in fact, isolated moorland communities. The research of Rod Lyon and others have contested the view that Pentreath was the last native speaker.[57] In fact, there is sufficient evidence that Cornish continued to be spoken for a long time after her death in areas further to the North and East. The Lizard, too, has been posited as another unrecognised pocket of survival. Lyon, in fact, demonstrates that there were a considerable number of Cornish speakers who existed beyond Dolly Pentreath's time, up until the turn of the eighteenth into the nineteenth century.[58] Cultural memory so it would seem, was allowing the language to succeed albeit 'secretly' and often beyond the will and intention of observers, recorders and collectors. It has been noted by sociolinguists that this secret 'ecology' in a language's final stages of operation, is often observed.[59] Clearly because something is not recorded, it does not necessarily mean it was not taking place.

Likewise, the work of Emma Mitchell has shown that in contrast to much traditional knowledge, many of the nineteenth-century antiquarians who were studying and recording the last specimens of the language used Cornish as a way of articulating their own ideological agendas – among these that whilst Cornish was a convenient foundation myth for 'Great Britain', it was a vestigial inconvenience.[60] Its cultural memory made it as significant as perhaps the civilizations and languages of Rome and Greece, but they actually subscribed to the dominant cultural force: English.[61] In this way, such antiquarians were already beginning to manipulate wider cultural memory by emphasising the language's 'extinction'. Not only did this pave the way for modernity but also helped to fossilise notions of 'Celticity'. Thus it was generally deemed sensible that the language had not survived, a view expressed not too many years earlier by observers such as Davies Gilbert,[62] and perhaps even as far back as the writings of Richard Carew.[63]

Paradoxically, this tradition of scholarship did have ramifications on aspects of the Cornish Revival and by implication, later academic scholarship on Cornish. In the former, it is curious that for many years some of the Revivalists broadly ignored this period in favour of the Medieval Age (perhaps because this is where the 'true' literature was to be found so that Cornwall might compete on a pan-Celtic level) . For example, in the whole of Robert Morton Nance's work on the language, he tended to give short shrift to the 'Late' texts and to successive possible speakers.[64] In addition, A.S.D. Smith in 1947 offerd very little on later speakers and writers who emerge after Edward Lhuyd c.1700.[65] Jenner, although intrigued by these late speakers, and survivals,[66] and operating in an age where notation and conversation was possible, did not always seemingly find the time to seek them out.[67]

To a certain extent, the Revivalists' overall agenda (Jenner perhaps excepted) is a precursor of the present Kemmyn group of scholars and researchers who have an ideological agenda which sees their form of the language as more 'genuinely Celtic' and

The home of the Keigwin family in Mousehole. The plaque on the wall commemorates the Spanish attack in 1595 when this was the only house not destroyed (Photograph by Sarah Chapman)

accurate in pronunciation and spelling.[68] Clearly, part of the notion is that the cultural memory of the revived language is best taken from a period when the language was (in the memory of this group's view) 'uncorrupted' and possibly 'un-Anglicised'. For this group Mousehole's wider antiquity was not old enough. Mousehole, in this mindset, would be too modern, and such a group was seeking their revived form of the language from the cultural memory of the 'pure' Medieval period. It was looking to other landscapes and places for its inspiration: Glasney College, the culture of *plen-an-gwarries* and the everyday life of the pre-modern Celto-Catholic period.[69]

Likewise, for the groups of speakers of Cornish interested in this Late period, Mousehole was a place adorned with important cultural memory, since it held much of the corpus and significant figures of this later phase of the language. Mousehole was also sufficiently modern, working-class and perhaps also Protestant enough to reflect the ideological concerns of this group – that the language should be prised out of the fist of 'Medievalism'. The fact that there were figures above and beyond those such as Pentreath and Bodinar only enhanced their iconic status in being the last resistance before effectively becoming dispossessed.[70] Mousehole's status as a working port, with many valued Cornish credentials also gave the late presence of the language a kind of validity that it had struggled with for much of the modern era.[71] The language was also ironically operating in a location which in the twentieth century was becoming an icon of tourist Cornwall (visitors being attracted to the picturesque streets, quaint cottages and curious ope-ways).

Whatever the on-going arguments about authenticity of different 'dialects' or 'registers' of Cornish and whether enough speakers survived post-Pentreath to make the language operational, of late there has been another shift in the perceived 'Celtic detachment' of Mousehole. Initiated by the scholarship of Robert Morton Nance, in re-inventing the 'Tom Bawcock's Eve' song, the tune has now become 'traditional'.

Nance, providing the song for Ralph Dunstan's 1932 anthology commented that in fact it was a piece of 'conjectural description' (a phrase really meaning that he made it up from scratch):

A merry plaace you may believe, was Mouzel 'pon Tom Bawcock's Eve.
To be there who wudn' wesh, to sup o' sibm soorts o' fesh!
When morgy brath had clear'd the path, Comed lances for a fry
And then we had a bit of scadm An starry gazy pie![72]

Although the song became known to some groups in the village in the post-war period (among them the Old Cornwall Society), the song was by no means widely known. It was only occasionally sung, although it was to have a far greater influence in its later cultural life. At the end of the twentieth century Mousehole found itself in a new position where its cultural memory was dictated by a new literary and ritual landscape. Antonia Barber and Nicola Bayley's beautifully illustrated children's book *The Mousehole Cat* (1990) redefined both the telling of the story of Tom Bawcock (the story takes Tom Bawcock's cat's perspective on events) and how the past community is conceived.[73] Far from being an epicentre of the Cornish language, this aspect of identity is displaced as the story is resoundingly 'English' in its telling. *The Mousehole Cat* is a best-selling children's book and one that is constantly in demand by tourists who visit the village. The narrative is a 'universal' story of resistance in the face of famine but given a localisation; a localisation that has now had over twenty years of considerable impact.

There has been further dispossession however. During the 1990s, moves were made in the community on the night of Tom Bawcock's Eve (23 December) to more publically celebrate the story and its folklore. Over a period of time, this involved singing Nance's re-constructed version of the song (the more extreme Anglo-Cornish of the verses modified), the school-children of the village developing a lantern parade (in which the lanterns constructed would resemble Tom, his boat and the famous 'seven sorts of fish') and in which these would be set upon the water inside the harbour. The latest development of this ritual is to combine the floating lanterns with air-borne and controversial Chinese lanterns.[74] Although the collective memory of the village broadly believes this invented tradition is something that has always happened, my research with individual members of Mousehole Old Cornwall Society tells a different story. The memory here is that 'nothing like that ever happened on Tom Bawcock's Eve when I was a girl' and that 'twas all invented by Kneehigh Theatre and the like'. Another informant told me that 'it 'ave got nothun to do with we – tis all incomers who set ut up'.[75] Therefore, for the older members of the community, the present celebrations are seen as cultural invention and perhaps even cultural imperialism.[76] Regardless as to whether the Tom Bawcock's Eve celebrations are a marker of community celebration and memory, events in the village do fit into a broader pattern of festival behaviour which defines modern Cornwall.[77] Such lanterns are seen in many other communities in Cornwall; most noticeably at present in Truro's spectacular City of Lights event.[78] There is an irony in the way in which this festival has been 'ingrained' or rather 'grafted' onto the community of Mousehole. The primitive lanterns constructed by the children of the community are purported to be organic and 'traditional' but are, in fact, invention. However, one might argue that Tom Bawcock's Eve is a powerful demonstration of the speed and vitality of the interface between community and collective memory. Perhaps even the 'misinformation' regarding the legacy of Cornish language has prompted the community to seek a new variant of their history in order to show cultural defiance. We may go further and argue that even if the older members of the community regard the festival as developed by 'incomers' and 'Kneehigh Theatre' its effect as a mechanism of resistance and celebration of the Mousehole community has been most effective. In this respect Mousehole follows many of the principles of Benedict Anderson's classic model of an 'imagined community' – one which territorialises itself and actively creates new community memory.[79]

Conclusion: Callin' un Home versus the Ingrained in Cornwall

Memory is something of a nebulous concept for many observers, and yet as we have seen, it offers a radical and important insight into the lasting effects of cultural displacement and dispossession, as well as understanding survival and renegotiation of ethnicity and identity in Cornwall. Cultural place-making may be hidden or obscured for the bulk of the observing population (as in the case of locations such as Demeliock and Castle-an-Dinas) as the result of dominant and often aggressive literary and folkloric activity elsewhere. That said, the degree to which this is 'ingrained' into both the memory and landscape of the territory is as ever, dependent on matters of education and the dissemination of information to recipients of the culture (be they indigenous or visiting). A recent children's history of Cornwall took a traditional, one might even say, 'anglicised' line when it came to re-telling the links between memory, landscape and culture, with Castle-an-Dinas again marginalised.[80]

Callin' 'ome the significance of Mousehole requires an alternative perspective on memory and place in Cornwall. One's view of the place is dependent on one's ideological perspective. For supporters of, say, the Kemmyn 'dialect' of Cornish, Mousehole may represent a vestigial and interesting footnote in the overall pantheon of Cornish: the Cornish used by speakers and writers there at the end of the eighteenth century a kind of 'corrupted' and perhaps even anglicised version of a once great Celtic language. For supporters of Late Cornish, Mousehole is perhaps viewed through a different lens – not only as one of the last bastions of survival of the language but also a wider symbol of the language lasting into the modern era in other parts and communities in Cornwall. For both groups, icons such as Dolly Pentreath are difficult mis-symbols to be 'corrected' and managed within the landscape. Mousehole is also part of a Cornwall-wide engagement with festival events and has reconfigured its heritage to fit the organic, 'child-friendly' and narrative basis of much contemporary leisure time. Although the Arthurian and 'Mouzel' may seem at distance to each other, in fact there is much from each interface of memory and place that is frighteningly similar. The Cornish must not be afraid to call home more and make sure the 'ingrained' continues to survive. Otherwise, as cultural geography warns, the dispossession and displacement grows all too easily.

Notes

1. See P. Shurmer-Smith and K. Hannam, *Worlds of Desire, Realms of Power: A Cultural Geography* (London, 1994); W. Norton, *Cultural Geography: Environments, Landscapes, Identities, Inequalities* , Oxford, 2005; J. Anderson, *Understanding Geography: Places and Traces*, London, 2009.
2. For the geo-political, see for example, B, Deacon, *Cornwall: A Concise History*, Cardiff, 2007; J. Angarrack, *Our Future is History: Identity, Law and the Cornish Question*, Bodmin, 2002. For the geo-linguistic, see, for example, P. Payton, 'Identity, Ideology and Language in Modern Cornwall' in H.L.C. Tristram (ed.), *The Celtic Englishes* , Heidelberg, 1997, pp.100-22; A.M. Kent, 'Bringing the Dunkey down from the Carn: Cornu-English in Context, 1549-2005 – A Provisional Analysis' in H.L.C. Tristram (ed.), *The Celtic Englishes* IV, Potsdam, 2005, pp.6-33.
3. S. Schama, *Landscape and Memory*, London, 2004.
4. P. J. Stewart and A. Strathern (eds.), *Landscape, Memory and History: Anthropological Perspectives*, London, 2003. See also A. S. Leoussi and S. Grosby (eds.), *Nationalism and Ethnosymbolism: History, Culture and Ethnicity in the Formation of Nations*, Edinburgh, 2007.
5. See R. Perks and A. Thomson (eds.), *The Oral History Reader*, London, 2006; L. Abrams, *Oral History Theory*, London, 2011; S. Trower (ed.), *Place, Writing and Voice in Oral History*, Basingstoke, 2011.
6. A. M. Kent, "In Some State...": A decade of the literature and literary studies of Cornwall' in P. Payton (ed.), *Cornish Studies: Ten*, Exeter, 2002, pp.212-39.
7. See for example, R. C. Carswell (ed.), *Mannaman's Cloak: An Anthology of Manx Literature*, London, 2010; Antonio Raúl de Toro Santos (ed.) *Breogán's Lighthouse: An Anthology of Galician Literature*, London, 2010; N.J. Goetzfridt (ed.), *Indigenous Literature of Oceania: A Survey of Criticism and Interpretation*, Westport, Connecticut, 1995.
8. See for example, L. Merton (ed.), *Thus Es Et: An Anthology of Cornish Dialect*, London, 2011; A. M. Kent, *The Hope of Place: Selected Poems in English 1990-2010*, London, 2010. Another less 'literary' but useful fusion of cultures is found in Sharron P. Schwartz, *Mining a Shared Heritage: Mexico's Little Cornwall / La Minería Patrimonio Compartido: El Pequeño Cornwall De México*, Cornwall, 2011.
9. A. C. Symons, 'Jack Clemo's Mystical Erotic Quest' in P. Payton (ed.), *Cornish Studies: Thirteen*, Exeter, 2005, pp.70-97; G. Goodman. 'Seeing the Clay Country: The Novels of Jack Clemo' in P. Payton (ed.), *Cornish Studies: Seventeen*, Exeter, 2009, pp.34-50.
10. P. Payton, 'John Betjeman and the Holy Grail: One Man's Celtic Quest' in P. Payton (ed.), *Cornish Studies: Fifteen*, Exeter, 2007, pp.185-208; P. Payton, *John Betjeman and Cornwall: The Celebrated Cornish Nationalist*, Exeter, 2010; C. Brace, 'Cornish Identity and Landscape in the Work of Arthur Caddick' in P. Payton (ed.), *Cornish Studies: Seven*, Exeter, 1999, pp.130-46.
11. E. Lavan, 'The Stage of the Nation in Medieval Cornwall' in P. Payton (ed.), *Cornish Studies: Eighteen*, Exeter, 2010, pp.182-78; B. Murdoch, 'Rex David, Bersabe, and Syr Urry: A Comparative Approach to a Scene in the Cornish Origo Mundi' in P. Payton (ed.), *Cornish Studies: Twelve*, Exeter, 2004, pp.288-304.
12. P. Payton (ed.), *Cornish Studies: Nineteen*, Exeter, 2011, p.1.
13. Core texts here include T. Brown and R. Stephens (eds.), *Nations and Relations: Writing Across the British Isles*, Cardiff, 2000; A. Aughey, *Nationalism, Devolution and the Challenge to the United Kingdom State*, London, 2001; H. Dix, *After Raymond Williams: Cultural Materialism and the Break-Up of Britain*, Cardiff, 2008; J. Kerrigan, *Archipelagic English: Literature, History, Politics 1603-1707*, Oxford, 2008.
14. B. Deacon, D. Cole and G. Tregidga, *Mebyon Kernow and Cornish Nationalism*, Cardiff, 2003. See also M. W Tschirschky, *Die Erfindung der Kerltischen Nation Cornwall: Kultur, Identität und ethnischer Nationalismus in der britischen Peripherie*, Heidelberg. 2006.
15. See, for example, Anthony Gibson, *With Magic in My Eyes: West Country Literary Landscapes*, Bath, 2011; Michael Williams, *Writers in Cornwal,* Redruth, 2010. Both texts fail to take notice of any developments in Cornish literary studies from 1990 to 2010.
16. See, for example, O. Padel (ed.), *W.M.M. Picken: A Medieval Cornish Miscellany*, Chichester, 2000, 'Oral and literary culture in medieval Cornwall' in H. Fulton (ed.), *Medieval Celtic Literature and Society*, Dublin, 2005, pp.95-116. Padel, has, in fact, been almost universally dismissive of the political dimension of contemporary Cornish Studies. This was reflected in the November 2010 series of three lectures he gave at the Royal Institution of Cornwall, Truro.
17. Witness the 'Centre' embracing Cornish Studies in, for example, 'The Creation of Cornwall' in *The Times Literary Supplement*, 6 January (2012), pp.12-13.

18. See, for example, A. Lupack (ed.), *Modern Arthurian Literature: An Anthology of English and American Arthuriana from the Renaissance to the Present*, New York, 1992; E. D. Kennedy (ed.), *King Arthur: A Casebook*, London, 2002.
19. For helpful historical and economic background, see J, Matingley, *Cornwall and the Coast: Mousehole and Newlyn*, Chichester, 2008.
20. See, for example, J. L. Palmer, *The Cornish Chough Through the Ages*, Cornwall, n.d.
21. Ceremonies of the Gorsedd of the Bards of Cornwall, Cornwall, n.d., pp.10-11. For background, see R. Lyon, *Gorseth Kernow/The Cornish Gorsedd: What it is and what it does*, Cornwall, 2008.
22. See, for example, A.S. Fredrick (ed. and trs.), *Beroul: The Romance of Tristan*, Harmondsworth, 1970; E. M. R. Ditmus, *Tristan and Iseult in Cornwall*, Brockworth, 1969.
23. Some key texts here have been Paul Broadhurst, *Tintagel and the Arthurian Mythos*, Launceston, 1992; Christine Poulson, *The Quest for the Grail: Arthurian Legend in British Arts 1840-1920*, Manchester, 1999, E. Archibald, and A. Putter (eds.), *The Cambridge Companion to Arthurian Legend*, Cambridge, 2009.
24. A. Kent, A. Hale and T. Saunders (eds. and trs.), *Inside Merlin's Cave: A Cornish Arthurian Reader 1000-2000*, London, 2000.
25. See B. K. Davison, *Tintagel Castle*, London, 1999. Weatherhill interestingly notes that in Italy it was common for the storyteller to preface his tale of the fantastical and supernatural with the words 'C'era una volta un castello in Cornovaglia [There was once a castle in Cornwall]'. See C. Weatherhill, *Myths and Legends of Cornwall*, Wilmslow, 1998, p.iii.
26. L. Thorpe (ed. and tr.) *Geoffrey of Monmouth: The History of the Kings of Britain*, Harmondsworth, 1966.
27. Ibid., p.51. On this, see the observations of Kent, Hale and Saunders, op.cit., pp.236-7.
28. C. Thomas, *Tintagel: Arthur and Archaeology*, London, 1993.
29. J.M. Gray (ed.), *Alfred, Lord Tennyson: Idylls of the King*, Harmondsworth, 1983; P. Brendon (ed.), *Robert Stephen Hawker: Cornish Ballads and Other Poems*, St Germans, 1975, pp.52-69; D. Hutchinson, *One Man's Dream: The Story of King Arthur's Great Halls*, Tintagel, 1999.
30. H. Jenner, 'Some Posssible Arthurian Place-Names in West Penwith' in *Journal of the Royal Institution of Cornwall*, Volume XIX (1912); H. Jenner, 'Tintagel Castle in History and Romance' in *Journal of the Royal Institution of Cornwall*, No.74 (1927).
31. C. Weatherhill, *A Concise Dictionary of Cornish Place-Names*, Cathai na Mart, 2009, p.23.
32. Ibid, p.ix-xviii.
33. Jenner, op.cit., (1927).
34. See William Hals, *The Complete History of Cornwall*, Truro, c/1736. A copy of the manuscript is held in the Courtney Library, Royal Institution of Cornwall, Truro. The relevant section is found in Kent, Hale and Saunders. op.cit., pp. 73-80.
35. See OS SW 944595.
36. See OS SW 951583.
37. See OS SW 946624. For a detailed examination of Castle-an-Dinas, see C. Weatherhill, *Cornovia: Ancient Sites of Cornwall and Scilly*, Penzance, 1985, pp. 114-6. See also C. Peters, *The Archaeology of Cornwall*, Fowey, 2005, p.134.
38. For background, see Kent, op.cit. (2010), pp. 229-48.
39. W. Stokes (ed. and tr.), *The Life of Saint Meriasek: Bishop and Confessor – A Cornish Drama*, London, 1872, pp.126-7.
40. P. Payton, "a concealed envy against the English': A Note on the Aftermath of the 1497 rebellions in Cornwall' in P. Payton (ed.), *Cornish Studies: One*, Exeter, 1993, p.4-13.
41. See http://cornishstannaryparliament.co.uk. Accessed 25 February 2012. See also Angarrack, op.cit., pp.250-74.
42. See G. Thomas and N. Williams (eds. and trs.) *Bewnans Ke/The Life of St Kea: A Critical Edition with Translation*, Exeter, 2007. For a consideration of the play, see Kent. op.cit., pp.248-63.
43. OS SX 004612.
44. Argued by Kent, Hale and Saunders. op.cit., pp. 13-34.
45. For a context see P.B. Ellis, *Celt and Saxon: The Struggle for Britain AD 410-937*, London, 1993.
46. D. Fowler, *The Life and Times of John Trevisa, Medieval Scholar*, Seattle, 1995.
47. For background, see J. Whetter, *The History of Glasney College*, Padstow, 1988.
48. For a discussion, see Kent, op.cit., pp.221-5.
49. For a perspective on this, see G. Busby and Z. Hambley, 'Literary Tourism and the Daphne du Maurier Festival' in P. Payton (ed.), *Cornish Studies: Eight*, Exeter, 2000, p.197-212.
50. See http://www.heartlandscornwall.com. Accessed 25 February 2012. See, for example, M. Combellack, *The Permanent History of Penaluna's Van*, Peterborough, 2003; A.M. Kent, *Voodoo Pilchard*, Wellington, 2010;
51. See *Daphne du Maurier Festival of Arts and Literature Programme*, Fowey, 2011.
52. See http://www.miracletheatre.co.uk. Accessed 26 February 2012. For the text, see Edward Bosenketh, *Tin*, London, 1888.
53. See the general pattern in C. Weatherhill, *Cornish Place Names and Language*, Wilmslow, 1995. The argument is established in numerous texts. See for example. P. B. Ellis, *The Cornish Language and its Literature*, London, 1974; P.A.S. Pool, *The Death of Cornish*, Cornwall, 1982. See also M. Spriggs, 'Where Cornish was Spoken and When: A Provisional Synthesis' in P. Payton (ed.), *Cornish Studies: Eleven*, Exeter, 2003, pp. 228-69.

54. For helpful background on these figures and their achievement, see A.M. Kent and T. Saunders (eds. and trs.), *Looking at the Mermaid: A Reader in Cornish Literature 900-1900*, London, 2000.
55. See M. Spriggs, 'The Three Epitaphs of Dolly Pentreath' in P. Payton (ed.), *Cornish Studies: Eighteen*, Exeter, 2010, pp. 203-224.
56. See, for example, R. A. J. Walling, *The West Country*, London, 1955, p.258; J. W. Lambert, *The Penguin Guides: Cornwall*, London, 1954, p.109.
57. R. Lyon, *Cornish: The Struggle for Survival*, Nancegollan, 2001; Weatherhill. op.cit., pp.147-48; S. Lowena, 'Charles Rogers's 'Vocabulary of the Cornish Language', the Rylands Vocabulary, and gatherers of pre-Revival fragments' in P. Payton (ed.), *Cornish Studies: Nineteen*, Exeter, 2011, pp.105-22. The work of R. Gendall has also been crucial in this field.
58. Ibid., p.22.
59. See S. S. Mufwene, *The Ecology of Language Evolution*, Cambridge, 2001; L. A. Grenoble and L. J. Whaley, *Saving Languages: An introduction to language revitalization*, Cambridge, 2006.
60. E. Mitchell, 'The Myth of Objectivity: The Cornish Language and the Eighteenth-Century Antiquarians' in P. Payton (ed.), *Cornish Studies: Six*, Exeter, 1998, pp. 62-80.
61. The ancient pedigree of Cornish is examined by a number of writers. See, for example, John Boson's 'Elegy on the Death of James Jenkins' cited in Kent and Saunders, op.cit., pp.240-1; R. Hunt, *Popular Romances of the West of England: First Series*, London, 1881, pp.44-6.
62. See D. Gilbert (ed.), *Mount Calvary, or, the History of the Passion, Death and Resurrection of Jesus Christ, written in Cornish (as it may be conjectured) some centuries past. Interpreted in English in 1682 by J. Keigwin*, London, 1826.
63. See R. Carew, 'The Excellency of the English Tongue' in F.R. Halliday (ed.), *Richard Carew of Antony 1555-1620: The Survey of Cornwall Etc*, London, 1953, pp.303-8.
64. One notable exception is R.M. Nance, 'When was Cornish Last Spoken Traditionally?' in *The Journal of the Royal Institution of Cornwall*, New Series, Volume VII, Part 1 (1975), pp.76-82. Nance also published occasional small articles in *Old Cornwall: Journal of the Old Cornwall Societies*. See, for example, R, M. Nance 'A Cornish Letter, 1711' in *Old Cornwall*, April (1926).
65. A.S.D. Smith. *The Story of the Cornish Language: Its Extinction and Revival*, Camborne, 1947, pp.10-11.
66. See M. Everson (ed.), Henry Jenner's *Handbook of the Cornish Language*, Cathar na Mart, 2010 [1904].
67. See the observations of contributors to D. R. Williams (ed.), *Henry and Katharine Jenner: A Celebration of Cornwall's Culture, Language and Identity*, London, 2004. Jenner was clearly talking to the right kind of informants who knew of tradition and folklore. See his contribution to W. Y. Evans-Wentz (ed.), *The Fairy Faith in Celtic Countries*, Oxford, 1911, pp.103-85.
68. The academic basis here is found in K. George, *The Pronunciation and Spelling of Revived Cornish*, Cornwall, 1986. See also P. Dunbar and K. George, *Kernewek Kemmyn: Cornish for the Twenty-First Century*, Cornwall, 1997.
69 This is an ideology often reflected in both the narrative themes of published materials and in terms of lettering, iconography and image. The overt Medievalism of the Cornish Language Board is perhaps only just beginning to shift.
70. For the influence and importance of Mousehole, see for example, R. Gendall, *The Language of Our Cornish Forefathers*, Cornwall, n.d.
71. See the observations on the status of Cornish in P. Payton and B. Deacon, 'The Ideology of Language Revival' in P. Payton (ed.), *Cornwall Since the War: The Contemporary History of a European Region*, Redruth, 1993, p.271-90.
72. R. Dunstan, *Cornish Dialect and Folk Songs*, Truro, 1932, p.7.
73. A. Barber and N. Bayley, *The Mousehole Cat*, London, 1990.
74. As witnessed by this author initially in December 2010 and subsequently in 2011.
75. Research conducted by author at a meeting of Mousehole Old Cornwall Society, 3 December 2010.
76. It appears that some members of Kneehigh Theatre helped to initiate the new festival in the mid-1990s.
77. For background to aspects of this ritual year festivity, see T. Deane and T. Shaw, *The Folklore of Cornwall*, Stroud, 2003. See also Kent, op.cit., (2010), pp. 52-148.
78. See http://www.trurocityoflights.com. Accessed 26 February 2012.
79. See B. Anderson, *Imagined Communities*, London, 1983.
80. P. Burns, *A Children's History of Cornwall*, Bath, 2011, p.13

Stratton to St Keverne: Sites of memory from the Early Modern period

Garry Tregidga

Introduction

In the general election of January 1910 the Hon. Thomas C. Agar Robartes, Liberal candidate for St Austell, made his appeal to the electorate with the slogan 'A Cornishman for Cornishmen'. He added that 'the chief characteristic of Cornishmen was their love of independence. As a nation we dislike being trampled on'.[1] It will be suggested in this chapter that such comments reflect a wider patriotic reading of Cornwall's past. Key historical conflicts, in particular the 1497 and 1549 Cornish rebellions and the Civil War of the 1640s, produced a cultural memory of communal resistance linked to symbolic words like 'defiance', 'independence' and 'rebellion' that still reinforces the language of popular protest in contemporary Cornwall. Issues of change and continuity are addressed in relation to the remembrance of rebellion from the Early Modern period down to the present. Underpinning these connections are a spatial network of 'memory places' stretching from the West Cornwall village of St Keverne, the epicentre of the 1497 rebellion, to Civil War sites like Stratton in North Cornwall. In a contemporary context this is investigated through reference to the 500th anniversary celebrations of 1497 when cultural and political activists in the Cornish movement retraced the route of the rebellion from its start at St Keverne to eventual defeat at Blackheath on the outskirts of London.

Remembering Resistance: Cornwall and the Politics of Cultural Memory

The opening decades of the twentieth century form a pivotal period for Celtic politics. In Ireland the dramatic breakthrough of Sinn Fein following the Easter rising of 1916 culminated in the creation of the Irish Free State just six years later. Although Scotland and Wales continued to be governed from Westminster, the formation of Plaid Cymru in 1925 and the National Party of Scotland (predecessor of the Scottish National Party) in 1928 highlighted a growing desire for political autonomy. In contrast the Celto-Cornish Revival at this time can be regarded as an essentially non-political phenomenon. Emerging out of an essentially antiquarian interest in the Cornish language the early Revivalists focused on the creation of a series of cultural organisations notably Cowethas Kelto-Kernuack in 1901, the Federation of Old Cornwall Societies in 1924 and Gorseth Kernow in 1928. A political agenda was only adopted in 1951 with the launch of Mebyon Kernow (Sons of Cornwall). Crucially, this meant that nationalist activists in more recent decades have been unable to draw on a recent tradition of militant protest expressed through reference to local 'sites of memory'. Treve Crago makes a similar point. He concludes 'that the activities of the Cornish Movement have been "soft" in regards to the nature of their "nationalist" activities. So that while, in the recent ["hard"] history of most other Celtic nations, there exist symbolic events of resistance against the authority of the central state: Ireland its Easter uprising of 1916; Wales the burning of the Phwelli bombing school 1936; Brittany the destruction of the Honte statue in Rennes 1932; in contrast Cornwall lacks such a definite nationalist landmark of resistance'.[2]

Yet the distant past can also play an important part in the politics of cultural memory. A good example is Owain Glyndwr's uprising in Wales in the early 1400s since it provided a crucial inspiration for the development of Welsh nationalism in the 1890s.[3] By adopting this longer time span a useful comparison can be made with Cornwall. In 1953, for example, Dick Gendall claimed that there was a need for historians to recognise the separate identity of areas like Cornwall when studying the past. He added that 'Our bloody battles are not Hastings, Agincourt and Crecy, but Hingston Down and Slaughter Bridge, Fenny Bridge and Blackheath'.[4] In recent years there has been a renewed desire to ensure that the 'national' history of Cornwall is remembered. The campaign of John Angarrack is a good example of this radical 'Kernowcentric' approach since he believes that both archaeological and historical research on Cornwall is subject to political manipulation by a range of external organisations from English Heritage to the Church of England. Archaeological findings, he concludes, are explained with misleading terminology in order 'to obscure Celtic Cornwall's non-English roots', while Cornish children are 'compelled to attend a programme of education that indoctrinates them with English historical revisionism'.[5] Angarrack added that Cornish people 'should not be expected to remain passive observers while the memory of those who gave their lives in the struggle for Cornish national survival is defiled'.[6] The cultural significance of the act of remembering is also evident in Pol Hodge's bi-lingual study of the Prayer Book Rebellion of 1549. Echoing a House of Lords appeal ruling in the 1980s, Hodge concluded that as an ethnic group the Cornish possess 'a long-shared history, of which the group is conscious as distinguishing it from other groups, and the memory of which it keeps alive'.[7]

Hodge's reference to 1549 is significant since it is the Early Modern period that provides the focus for the remembrance of Cornish resistance to the English state. This sense of cleavage has been highlighted in scholarly debate with Bernard Deacon claiming that the Tudor period has 'become the principal battlefield of Cornish historiogra-

Memorial commemorating the Civil war battle at Stratton in 1643 (Photograph by Stanley Tregidga)

phy'.[8] On one side there is a critical view by historians like Ian Arthurson and John Chynoweth who claim that local events merely reflected wider trends.[9] While others like Philip Payton and Mark Stoyle stress the underlying importance of Cornish identity at this time. From this perspective the 1497 uprising led by Michael Joseph, a blacksmith (translated into Cornish as 'An Gof') from St Keverne on the Lizard, and Thomas Flamank, a lawyer from Bodmin, was an ethnic response to greater centralisation. It was provoked not just by extra taxation but by the suspension of the Stannaries in the previous year, thereby undermining Cornish autonomy and revealing existing cultural tensions in the periphery.[10] This pivotal event created a culture of rebellion with a second uprising in 1497 in support of Perkin Warbeck's claim to the throne. It was to be followed by Cornwall's militant reaction to the Protestant Reformation when the imposition of a new Prayer Book in English in 1549 resulted in yet another incursion into Devon. The Cornish rebels, in alliance with the Catholics of mid-Devon, besieged Exeter for several weeks before their eventual defeat. Once again there appeared to be an ethnic dimension evident in the rebel statement that 'we will have our old service in Latin, not in English, as it was before. And so we the Cornishmen (whereof certain of us understand no English) utterly refuse this new English'.[11] Stoyle adds that the Civil War period of the 1640s 'resurrected the ancient ethnic fault line in the South West' with the Cornish, despite rebelling against Royalist authority on previous occasions, now taking the side of the crown. Cornwall's paradoxical stance can be explained on the grounds that many of its inhabitants were still motivated by local factors:

> As England broke down into Civil War, thousands of Cornishmen rose up against the supporters of Parliament and ejected them from their county. This demonstration of support for the King was partly founded on a deep distaste for the intolerant, zealously Protestant form of Englishness which seemed to be the mark of the Parliamentarians. The 1642 rising drew on the same cultural anxieties as the Tudor revolts which had proceeded it ... Roundhead propagandists drew the appropriate parallels, specifically likening the 1642 rising to that of

1549, and denouncing the King's Cornish adherents as 'rebels'.[12]

However, a greater understanding of the 'rebellious' strand to Cornish identity can only be established by going beyond the conventional concept of objective historical debate. As Robert Gildea pointed out, 'the past is constructed not as fact but as myth' resulting in contrasting interpretations of events serving 'the interest of a particular community' in the present.[13] Indeed, there is a need to recognise the way in which both academic and popular writers have created a series of competing narratives over time. Subtle changes in language, combined with the discovery in some cases of new empirical evidence, can lead to fresh interpretations reflecting the fluid concerns of a community in transition. In a Cornish context this can be seen in relation to the emergence of the cult of Trelawny in the nineteenth century. Robert Stephen Hawker's patriotic *Song of the Western Men* written in 1825 was apparently based on an earlier fragment of a song commemorating Sir John Trelawny's imprisonment in the Tower of London in 1628. Hawker's mythical setting of events at the time of James II's imprisonment of Bishop Jonathan Trelawny in 1688 became immensely popular. Emerging as Cornwall's principal 'soul stirring patriotic' anthem it reinforced its image as a land of rebellion. Yet at the same time, according to Deacon, *Song of the Western Men* is a 'striking example of interpreting Cornish patriotism within a Protestant English identity'.[14] By the time of Cornwall's rugby success at Twickenham in 1991 'Trelawny' had been co-opted into popular culture as the central icon of 'resistance' and 'national' identity. Payton writing in 1996 observed that this was at the expense of figures associated with earlier events:

> Today, when Cornish rugby supporters are known as 'Trelawny's Army', and when these supporters at Twickenham ... sported 'Trelawny's Second Invasion' sweatshirts, it is ironic that it is Trelawny's non-rebellion that is routinely celebrated while 1497 and 1549 have generally slipped from public view.[15]

Just one year later, however, the 500th anniversary celebrations of the 1497 rebellion saw a renewed focus on these earlier events. It included a high-profile public history demonstration with a re-enactment of the 365 mile march of the Cornish rebel army from St Keverne in the west of Cornwall to the site of their eventual defeat at Blackheath near London. Entitled Keskerdh Kernow ('Cornwall Marches On'), the walk was linked to a range of cultural and educational activities that celebrated the distinctive identity and socio-economic concerns of Cornwall. Significantly, this popular commemoration ran alongside the vigorous academic debate between historians referred to earlier.

'A smith of these parts': Cultural and Spatial Narratives of Rebellion

But in order to tell the full story of 'rebellion' it is necessary to investigate its changing narratives through time. The remembrance of resistance by an ethnic community can be based on a variety of sources. Oral traditions and written texts are important, if at times conflicting, routes for sustaining a link with the past. Similarly, public commemorations of historic events, such as national victories and tragedies, offer a means of communicating the key identification symbols of ethnic groups. A sense of place can obviously assist this process since specific historic sites and monuments create visible markers, thereby creating meaning for future generations. Burial mounds, for example, instantly link the past with the present by acting as physical 'reminders of the glory of heroes' from a previous age.[16] In this section consideration will be given to these various mediums of transmission in a Cornish context.

Oral tradition is perhaps the most obvious way of maintaining a memory culture. This was particularly the case during the essentially pre-literate era when the 'rebellious' image of the Cornish emerged. Indeed, it can be argued that the 'commotions' of the Tudor period need to be discussed in the context of the earlier struggles between Cornish and Saxon. Gail Berlin points out that 'a good memory was a valued possession' in the early medieval period. Even literate members of society saw the process of memorisation as a useful device for preserving knowledge of a community's early history.[17] The power of oral tradition in sustaining a mythical construction of Cornish identity is most evident in regard to the popular legend of King Arthur. As a fifteenth century writer observed, 'Bretons and Cornish sayeth thus, that Arthur levyth yet ... and shall come and be a king again'.[18] The strength of feeling on this subject had been demonstrated quite clearly some 300 years earlier when the Cornish apparently attacked a group of French clerics in Bodmin for suggesting that Arthur was dead.[19] Myths and legends retained such an emotive appeal for the Cornish since these tales were a way of symbolising issues grounded in reality. In the case of Arthur it has been claimed by Stoyle that 'such predictions were not just idle fancies, but reflected the latent desire of a conquered Celtic people to revenge themselves upon their oppressors and regain their lost independence'.[20] The turn of the seventeenth century witnessed a renewed interest in the life and customs of Cornwall by chroniclers and cartographers who recorded their observations of the Duchy's inhabitants.[21] Although the Cornish had been forced to accept the River Tamar as the border in 936 AD, it is intriguing that the use of oral-based evidence by these contemporary observers suggests that the Cornish still had bitter memories of their expulsion from South-West England well into the Early Modern period. John Norden, who visited the region in the 1590s and in the following decade became the senior surveyor to the Duchy of Cornwall, remarked that the inhabitants of Cornwall 'retain a kind of concealed envy against the English, whom they yet affect with a desire of revenge for their fathers sakes, by whom their fathers received the repulse'.[22] Richard Carew, a landowner from East Cornwall, made a similar observation in his *Survey of Cornwall* in 1602:

> One point of their former roughness some of the western people do yet retain, and therethrough in some measure verify that testimony which Matthew of Westminster giveth of them together with the Welsh, their ancient countrymen, namely, how fostering a fresh memory of their expulsion long ago by the English, they second the same with a bitter repining at their fellowship; and this the worst sort express in combining against and working them all the shrewd turns which with hope of impunity they can devise.[23]

In both extracts memory can be seen as the critical factor in creating an underlying sense of hostility towards the English. Norden talks plainly in genealogical terms of 'a desire of revenge for their fathers sakes', while Carew points to the 'memory of their expulsion long ago by the English'. This is significant since it suggests that the legacy of Cornwall's resistance to the Saxons provided the cultural framework for the events of 1497 and 1549. It has been claimed that memory is not a static process, with Cornelius Holtorf pointing out that 'the past is actively constructed depending on certain social and mental conditions'.[24] One might argue that Carew's comments indicate that the dramatic events of the Tudor period were literally responsible for 'fostering a fresh memory' of the Duchy's past. An underlying sense of grievance towards the English was accentuated as the outcome of the Tudor rebellions created an extra layer of remembering to be passed on by means of oral communication to future generations. These rebellions then provided the background for perceptions of identity in the Civil War of the 1640s. The success of the Cornish forces in battles throughout the South West of Britain stimulated memories of the 'commotions' of the previous century on the part of the parliamentarians and was perhaps regarded as yet another opportunity by the Cornish Royalists to obtain revenge for their earlier expulsion from Dumnonia by the Saxons. It certainly appears that many Cornish regarded the Civil War from a local perspective. By the mid-1640s the Cornish people saw the future King Charles II as an independent Duke in his own right in line with earlier traditions and it was claimed that there was 'a common muttering among [them] that their country was never conquered'.[25]

Yet subsequent events were to weaken this underlying sense of identity continuity. The shift from an oral to a text-based society was to privilege the Cornish experience in the 1640s at the expense of the Tudor rebellions. In the first place books written after the Restoration in 1660 reflected the emergence of an orthodox Royalist tradition that tended to downplay any suggestion that the Cornish had fought the war in defence of their own interests as they had done in previous 'commotions'. The Earl of Clarendon's *History of the Rebellion*, completed in the 1670s but published in the early 1700s, was a symbol of this subtle reconstruction of the past. Based partly on Clarendon's own experiences during the Civil War it offered an official narrative based on Cornwall's ultra loyalty to the crown. Stoyle concluded that 'as the generation of the 1640s gradually died away, and as impressions of the Civil War came, of necessity, to be founded on the authority of written sources ... rather than on that of personal recollection', a major theme of Cornish cultural identity was defused.[26] Written accounts were reinforced by a 'landscape of remembrance'. A series of stone monuments at sites associated with local Royalists like the Grenville family, combined with copies of the famous 1643 letter of thanks from King Charles I in parish churches in the Duchy, provided visual reminders for the new myth of Cornish loyalty. Stoyle points out that in the eighteenth and nineteenth centuries key sites of memory like the battlefield of Stratton and Kilkhampton Church became 'recognized stopping-off points along what was, in effect, a tourist trail through "the Grenville Country" of north-east Cornwall'.[27]

This contrasted significantly with the way in which the Tudor rebellions were remembered. Although the events of both 1497 and 1549 continued to be recorded in written accounts of Cornwall's past, it was not until the middle decades of the twentieth century that a new generation of writers began to subtly alter these narratives in line with wider cultural and historical trends. Carew's *Survey of Cornwall* is an appropriate text to start with since he provided a basic narrative that tended to be copied by writers in subsequent centuries and his treatment of the Tudor rebellions is a good example. In the first place it is interesting that Carew appears to emphasise the general rebellious instincts of the Cornish. Apart from referring to the Prayer Book rebellion as the 'Cornish commotion', he noted that there had been disenchantment with central government back in the reign of Richard III and that this tension had re-emerged by 1497:

> Neither did his suppressor and successor, Henry the Seventh, find them loyal; for the Cornishmen, repining at a subsidy lately granted him by act of parliament, were induced to rebellion by Thomas Flammock, a gentleman, and Michael Joseph, a blacksmith ... In the same fatal year of revolts, Perkin Warbeck, a counterfeit prince, landed in Cornwall, went to Bodmin, assembled a train of rake-hells, assaulted Exeter, received the repulse, and in the end sped, as is known, and as he deserved.[28]

An obvious point to make is there is no micro sense of place in Carew's discussion of the first rebellion. The western origins of the rebellion at St Keverne are not even mentioned, while Joseph, now regarded as the key figure in the uprising, is effectively given secondary importance alongside Flamank or 'Flammock'. It was left to William Hals (1655-1737) to provide a spatial context for events. Yet in his parochial survey, first published in 1750 and subsequently republished by later writers, he ignored St Keverne and pointed instead to Bodmin with Joseph described as 'a smith of those parts'.[29] In 1814 the Rev Daniel Lysons and his brother Samuel were still describing An Gof as a blacksmith from Bodmin.[30] C.S. Gilbert in 1817 stressed the importance of the town as a centre of rebellion in the Tudor period with only passing reference to Joseph and again no mention of St Keverne. Instead Gilbert pointed to the traditional role of 'Castle Kynock' as the 'spot appointed for the assembly of the disaffected, who flocked in from all quarters of the shire, to range themselves under the rebel standard' in 1549 just as rebel forces had assembled there in the Warbeck uprising. Bodmin was still regarded as the focus for insurrection in the first half of the twentieth century.[31] Even writers associated with the growing interest in Cornish culture and history like Thurstan Peter in 1906 and the Rev Sabine Baring-Gould in 1910 simply repeated earlier statements including, in the case of the latter, the assumption that Joseph was a blacksmith from the old capital of Cornwall.[32]

This had significant implications for the spatial dimension to Cornwall's landscape of remembrance. The focus was clearly on the rural and romantic parishes in the east and north stretching from Castle Kynock at Bodmin to the civil war sites of the subsequent century around Stratton. One might add that the Arthurian traditions associated with places like Tintagel, Slaughterbridge near Camelford and Dozmary Pool on Bodmin Moor reinforced this geographical concentration. West Cornwall, in contrast, lacked any visible reminders or public commemorations. Arguably, this only began to change in 1860 when Prince Lucien Bonaparte's memorial to Dolly Pentreath was

1997 statue depicting Thomas Flamank and Michael Joseph 'An Gof' at St Keverne (Photograph by Sarah Chapman)

erected in the village of Paul. Although not specifically related to the theme of rebellion, it did mean that there was now an opportunity for a wider spatial base to remembrance in Cornish culture. Closely associated with the growing interest in Cornwall's ancient language was the Rev Wladyslaw Somerville Lach-Szyrma, Anglican vicar of Newlyn from 1874-90. He played a key role in the centenary commemorations of Pentreath's death in 1877 and was a keen advocate of public ceremonies and memorials in general to foster a greater interest in the past. For example, he campaigned for the new Truro Cathedral to become 'a Cornish Westminster Abbey' with memorials both to the 'old Cornu-British kings' and more recent figures like Richard Trevithick and Humphrey Davey associated with the industrial culture of West Cornwall.[33] Although making just a passing reference to the secular events of 1497 in *A Church History of Cornwall*, it was noticeable that Lach-Szyrma highlighted the importance of the west in relation to what he termed Cornwall's 'religious war' of the late 1540s. In particular he depicted St Keverne, which he concluded was also the 'centre of the late rebellion of Henry Courtney' in 1537, as 'a place where the spirit of revolt was rife'. He linked events to 'the spirit of the next century, when Cornishmen cried out "And shall Trelawney die"' and described Sampford Courtney, where the rebels were defeated by forces loyal to the crown, as the 'last battle between the English and Cornish'.[34] Yet Lach-Szyrma appears to be a notable exception and following his move to Essex in 1890 there was no obvious advocate of the conscious memorialisation of the past.

Writers were generally reluctant in any case to commemorate Cornish resistance to the English establishment. Carew's comments about the 'train of rake-hells' that supported Warbeck reflect the embarrassment of Cornwall's Anglicised gentry in the Early Modern period. Drew in 1824 was still referring to those 'local commotions, in which Cornwall has had the dishonour of erecting the standard of rebellion'.[35] Perhaps reflecting the social and political tensions of the early decades of the nineteenth century it was noticeable that he also distinguished between the leaders of the first rebellion of 1497. Flamank was presented as an articulate and educated 'descendant of an ancient and wealthy family, whose name has appeared among the principal landholders' in the Bodmin area in 1255. By contrast, the 'primary motive by which Joseph professed to be actuated, was ambition' and he consequently paid for 'his crimes by the forfeiture of his life'.[36] It was more socially acceptable for Drew to remember Cornwall's 'loyalty' to the crown in the 1640s and he pointed to those Royalist 'officers, whose names will be remembered with veneration while the history of these transactions remain on our national records'.[37] Drew's background as a Methodist minister also influenced his reading of the past. He appears to suggest that Cornwall's reputation for 'local insurrections', presumably the food riots of the eighteenth and early nineteenth centuries, had emerged out of the earlier Cornish commotions. Only the rise of Methodism had been able to control the violent instincts of his Cornish countrymen:

> In the several rebellions by which Cornwall has been disgraced, and of which notice has been already taken, the same spirit has been displayed, and the same feature of character has been rendered conspicuous. In latter years its vigorous pulsations have been felt in local insurrections, from which many pernicious consequences have resulted. And if the range of its operations and its violence is now suppressed, and in many places subdued, these happy effects may be attributed to the mild and ameliorating influence of more pure principles, which the benevolent spirit of Christianity has diffused throughout the population of Cornwall in modern days.[38]

But there is a paradox to these historical accounts of the Cornish commotions. Carew and subsequent writers had created, albeit unconsciously in some cases, an ethnic interpretation of the past that could be traced back to the struggles between the Saxons and the Cornu-British. Drew is a good example since he concluded that the Tudor rebellions showed that the Cornish 'had not yet wholly lost that spirit of daring independence which their British forebears had transmitted to them'.[39] Educated audiences, both in Cornwall and elsewhere, had a basic understanding through historical surveys and travel guides of both Cornwall's Celtic past and the events of the Early Modern period. This process took place well before the official emergence of the Cornish Revival movement in the early twentieth century and it helps to explain Robartes's comments at the start of the chapter. Yet for this spirit of 'rebellion' to provide a sense of legitimacy for the cause of Cornish nationalism it required a greater politicisation of the embryonic Revivalist movement itself.

The Rise of An Gof

In retrospect the 1940s marked a key stage in the interpretation of Cornwall's rebellious past. Perhaps the pivotal moment occurred in 1941 with the publication of A.L. Rowse's *Tudor Cornwall*. Although Rowse had a complex 'relationship with Cornwall and the Cornish',[40] his use of language to explain the Age of Rebellion in his native land showed that it was now possible to impose new narratives on events.[41] Thus, Cornwall was presented as 'a remote Celtic-speaking province' that was being 'absorbed into the main stream of English life'. He added that 'the Rebellions of 1497 and 1549 were to Cornwall what the '15 and the '45 were to the Highlands'.[42] Moreover, as a result of his research for *Tudor Cornwall* Rowse was to highlight the importance of both Joseph and St Keverne:

> A letter of Sir William Godolphin's a generation later informs us that that the people began to stir first in the parish of St Keverne in the Lizard area, where dwelt Michael Joseph, the blacksmith, a man of great force and stout courage who became their leader. It is worth noting that St Keverne would fall within the sphere of the provost of Glasney as collector; it was a large populous parish which now started a tradition of unquietness.[43]

This historical reassessment took place within the context of a wider politicisation of the Cornish movement as new activists came to the fore. A good example is Helena Charles, who was shortly to become the first chairman of Mebyon Kernow. In 1949 she was already calling for the Cornish to defend their culture like their Breton 'cousins' in order to prevent 'assimilation to England'.[44] There was also a greater recognition at the time of the need to commemorate the past. In 1949 St Ives publicly marked the 400th anniversary of the Prayer Book rebellion with the local Roman Catholics unveiling a memorial plaque dedicated to John Payne, the local Portreeve who had been hung for supporting the rebel cause. The event was significant since it highlighted a spatial shift in memorialisation from east to west. Indeed, it was no coincidence that it took place in St Ives since in the late 1940s the town was at the forefront of the post-war Celtic Revival. In 1947 the St Ives Catholic Irish Association had been formed with a regular programme of Gaelic language classes, Celtic dancing, crafts and debates. The Cornwall School of Inter-Celtic Dancing was also officially based in St Ives and an Inter-Celtic Festival was held in the town in 1949 in association with Gorseth Kernow.[45]

1949 plaque commemorating the 1549 Prayer Book rebellion at St Ives' Roman Catholic church (Photograph by Sarah Chapman)

In the same year it was reported that support for the new *Cornish Review* magazine was concentrated in West Cornwall with a readership of 400 and 300 in St Ives and Penzance respectively.[46] Similarly, when Mebyon Kernow was formed in 1951 the inaugural meeting was held in the western industrial town of Redruth. Although Mebyon Kernow was eventually able to attract support in other parts of Cornwall, particularly at Padstow and Liskeard in the late 1960s,[47] the nationalist movement remained closely associated with the west. In 1975, for example, their competitors in the newly-formed Cornish Nationalist Party claimed that 'Mebyon Kernow has become practically limited to the west of Kernow. By far the majority of officers and executive representatives are from west of Truro'.[48]

These developments provide the framework for understanding the significance of the 1966 celebrations of the 1497 rebellion. It was apparently the first public commemoration of the uprising, and significantly was held in the west at St Keverne. Organised by Mebyon Kernow, the event attracted widespread support including the participation of Cornwall's leading councillors and MPs. An Gof had clearly now moved to the fore with Flamank considered to be of only secondary importance as a rebel leader. By the 1960s the 'Everyman' image of An Gof had a democratic and populist appeal that was summed up by Alderman Kimberley Foster, chairman of Cornwall County Council, who 'pointed out that Michael Joseph the Smith, an ordinary working man, had made a great decision, to protest against unjust taxation levied to finance a war against Scotland, another Celtic land'. Foster added that Cornwall needed the 'spirit of the Smith more than ever' at a time when its 'very existence' was threatened by the possible creation of a new tier of regional government based at Bristol.[49] The anti-tax nature of the rebellion meant that he could also be an iconic symbol for those individuals wishing to make a right-wing protest against socialism. A good example was Rowse, the person who had effectively rediscovered Michael Joseph through his historical research. Despite his political background as a Labour parliamentary candidate in the 1930s, in a letter to Mebyon Kernow at the time of the celebrations he combined the rhetoric of Cornish nationalism with a Poujadist attack on the state:

> All good Cornishmen must sympathize with the Smith's revolt against taxes imposed by the English! Especially when so much of the County's wealth was drained away through centuries by the Duchy for the upkeep of the English crown. Perhaps we need the spirit of the Smith again today to raise the standard against predatory over-taxation by the English state in aid of the slack and idle, the seedy and parasitic Welfare State.[50]

Moving forward in time the 500th anniversary celebrations of the 1497 rebellion offer further insight into the power of the past. Interestingly, the personal reflections of the modern-day marchers highlighted an essentially spiritual association with the historic sites of their ancestors, starting with impromptu ceremonies at places like Helman Tor during the march through Cornwall and ending at an unmarked mound at Blackheath that was reputed to be the mass grave of the rebels.[51] Once again the event took on added significance because of the widespread feeling that the marchers were also demonstrating against the perceived neglect of modern Cornwall by central government. The marchers even drew up the so-called Blackheath Declaration, which called for immediate measures to protect Cornwall's economy and culture. Alistair Quinnell, a county councillor from Bodmin who wrote the preface to the official commemorative publication of the event, was keen to emphasise the bonds between historical and contemporary Cornwall:

> Within these pages, the reader will detect the renewal of Cornish culture, language and identity, and the strength of pride and protest, the latter reflected in the Blackheath Declaration, focusing on today's beleaguered Cornish economy. There is an uncanny parallel of 'knowing the reason why', which justified the rebellion of 1497 led by Michael Joseph of St Keverne and Thomas Flamank of Bodmin and the economic situation and social deprivation of Cornwall today.[52]

Conclusion

Quinnell's comments show how the bond between memory and place can take on symbolic importance when it comes to the cultural and political concerns of contemporary society. This has been a critical factor in the changing imaginings of characters like An Gof, Flamank and Trelawney through the centuries. In the second half of the twentieth century the rediscovery of the Blacksmith of St Keverne, combined with the timely radicalisation of the Cornish movement, provided a new sense of historical legitimacy and popular appeal for nationalism that could build on the existing sense of 'rebellion' in Cornish culture. Underlying the rise of the An Gof cult was a spatial shift from east to west in Cornwall's landscape of cultural remembrance. By 1997 this process was to enable the emergence of a more confident and articulate sense of 'Cornishness' that could finally draw inspiration from the past in order to articulate a meaningful agenda for the future.

Notes

1. *West Briton*, 7 and 21 January 1910.
2. Treve Crago, 'Celtic Heroes? Illuminating Dark Narratives from the Shadows of Collaboration', unpublished conference paper, Berlin, 2004, p. 1.
3. E. Henken, *National Redeemer: Owain Glyndwr in Welsh Tradition*, University of Wales Press, 1996. See also G. Beiner, *Remembering the Year of the French: Irish Folk History and Social Memory*, University of Wisconsin Press, 2006.
4. *New Cornwall*, No. 8, May 1953.
5. John Angarrack, *Our Future is History: Identity, Law and the Cornish Question*, Independent Academic Press, 2002, p. 25 and 254.
6. *Ibid*, p. 69.
7. Pol Hodge, *Cornwall's Secret War – The True Story of the Prayer Book War/Bresel Gevrinek a Gernow – Hwedhel Gwir Bresel An Lyver Pysadow*, Kowethas an Yeth Kernewek, 1999, p. 18.
8. Bernard Deacon, 'Propaganda and the Tudor State or Propaganda of the Tudor Historians?', in Philip Payton (ed.), *Cornish Studies, Eleven*, University of exeter Press, 2003, p.317.
9. Ian Arthurson, '"As able we be to depose him": ... Rebellion in the South West, 1497' in Simon Parker (ed.), *Cornwall Marches On*, Keskerdh Kernow Limited, 1998, pp. 22-8; John Chynoweth, Tudor Cornwall, Tempus, 2002, pp. 21-31.
10. Philip Payton, '"a ... concealed envy against the English": a Note on the Aftermath of the 1497 Rebellions in Cornwall' in Philip Payton (ed.), *Cornish Studies: One*, University of Exeter Press, pp. 4-13; Mark Stoyle, 'Cornish Rebellions, 1497-1648' in Parker (ed.), *Cornwall Marches On*, p. 12.
11. Quoted in W.S. Lach-Szyrma, *A Church History of Cornwall and of the Diocese of Truro*, Netherton and Worth, Truro, 1889.
12. Mark Stoyle, *West Britons: Cornish Identities and the Early Modern British State*, University of Exeter Press, 2002, p. 24.
13. Robert Gildea, *The Past in French History*, Yale University Press, 1996.
14. Bernard Deacon, *Cornwall: A Concise History*, University of Wales Press, p. 149.
15. Philip Payton, *Cornwall*, Alexander Associates, 1996, p. 168.
16. Cornelius Holtorf, *Monumental Past*, http://citd.scar.utoronto.ca/CITDPress/holtorf/6.6.html
17. Gail Berlin, 'Memorization in Anglo-Saxon England: Some Case Studies' in W.F.H. Nicolaisen, *Oral Tradition in the Middle Ages*, Center for Medieval & Renaissance Studies, Binghamton, 1995, pp. 98-113; see also Mary Lynn Rampolla, '"A Pious Legend": St Oswald and the Foundation of Worcester Cathedral Priory' in Nicolaisen, *Oral Tradition*, p. 188.
18. F.J. Furnivall (ed.), *Arthur: A Short Sketch of his Life and History*, London, 1864, p. 19. Quoted in Stoyle, West Britons, p. 19.
19. Stoyle, *West Britons*, p. 19.
20. Stoyle, 'Cornish Rebellions', p. 10
21. Angarrack, Our Future is History, pp. 206-24.
22. John Norden, *Speculi Britanniae Pars: A Topographical and Historical Description of Cornwall*, William Pearson, London, 1728, p. 28
23. Richard Carew, *The Survey of Cornwall*, London, 1602, 953, p. 67.
24. Holtorf, *Monumental Past*, http://citd.scar.utoronto.ca/CITDPress/holtorf/2.0.html
25. Stoyle, *West Britons*, pp. 41, 44, 70, 86-9.
26. *Ibid*, pp. 168-9.
27. *Ibid*, pp. 157-83 and 175.
28. Carew, pp. 97-8.
29. Davies Gilbert, *The Parochial History of Cornwall*, Vol. 1, J.B. Nichols and Son, 1838, p. 86.
30. Rev Daniel Lysons and Samuel Lysons, *Magna Britannia*, Vol. 3 (Cornwall), London, 1814, p. xiii.
31. C.S. Gilbert, *An Historical Survey of the County of Cornwall*, Vol. 1, J. Congdon, 1817, pp. 13-6.
32. Thurstan C. Peter (ed.), A *Compendium of the History and Geography of Cornwall*, Netherton and Worth, Truro, 1906, p. 46. S. Baring-Gould, *Cornwall*, Cambridge University Press, 1910, p. 102.
33. *Royal Cornwall Gazette*, 9 November 1899.
34. Lach-Szyrma, *A Church History of Cornwall*, p. 79.
35. Samuel Drew and Fortescue Hitchens, *The History of Cornwall*, Vol. 1, Helston, 1824, p. 495.
36. *Ibid*, p. 481.
37. *Ibid*, p. 499.
38. *Ibid*, p. 711.
39. *Ibid*, p. 480.
40. Philip Payton, *A.L. Rowse and Cornwall: A Paradoxical Patriot*, University of Exeter Press, 2005, p. 8.
41. For an example of a nationalist narrative on the events of 1549 at this time see Ashley Rowe, '1549-1949: A Tribute to Heroes' in *The Cornish Review*, No. 2, Summer 1949, pp. 39-43.
42. A.L.Rowse, *Tudor Cornwall: Portrait of a Society*, Jonathan Cape, London, 1941, p.
43. *Ibid*, p. 121.

44. Helena Charles, 'The Chough and the Ermin' in *The Cornish Review*, No. 1, Spring 1949, p. 38.
45. *The Cornish Review*, No. 2, Summer 1949, pp. 3, 17 and 19.
46. *Ibid*, p. 17.
47. Bernard Deacon, Dick Cole and Garry Tregidga, *Mebyon Kernow and Cornish Nationalism*, Welsh Academic Press, p. 51.
48. *An Baner Kernewek*, Vol 1, Number 1, 1975, p. 2.
49. *New Cornwall*, Vol. 14, No. 1, Spring 1966, pp. 53-55.
50. *Ibid*, p. 55.
51. Simon Parker (ed), *Cornwall Marches On!*, Keskerdh Kernow Limited, 1998, pp. 44-60, 78, 84 and 89.
52. *Ibid*, p. 1.

Civic pride in Truro in the early nineteenth century

David Thomson

Civic pride is perhaps most associated with Northern industrial towns such as Bradford and Leeds, with images of grandiose town halls and heavyweight mayoral chains such as that worn by Peter Simple's fictional creation, Alderman Foodbotham, 'the 25-stone iron-watch-chained, crag-visaged, grim booted chairman of the Bradford City Tramways and Fine Arts Committee'.[1] In addition to splendid town halls these places boast statues of local luminaries and parks named after local benefactors. However, such benefactors did not provide all the finance for the civic trappings; in an age often characterised by suggestions of municipal tightfistedness ratepayers' money was expended upon civic symbolism. Sometimes this expenditure could have been considered an investment on behalf of the local commercial lifeblood but for many of the demonstrations of civic pride it is difficult to discern any potential return beyond local patriotism.

Before considering whether there were, or were not, examples of civic pride in Truro in the early nineteenth century, it is necessary to address the question: what is civic pride? Ideas of 'civic virtue' are outlined by Machiavelli, drawing on notions of 'civic humanism' espoused by Aristotle. Clearly, given the circumstances of their authorship, such ideas relate to the governance of City States rather than the local administration of transport and open spaces but they are underpinned by notions of civic duty that connect with the matter in question. Asa Briggs, in different works, refers to 'city pride' and 'civic duty'.[2] The former relates to a belief held by many residents of the newly expanded towns, filthy health hazards though such places were, that they enjoyed a greater freedom than their country cousins; freedom from aristocratic influence and from the dead hand of tradition. Rapid growth also created an impression of vitality that was lacking in rural areas. Although Truro's expansion hardly compares to that of Manchester it is certainly possible to detect such 'city pride' in Truro in this period, in the political and religious reform movements that reviled aristocratic influence and revered the sense of the modern. But this 'city pride' does not quite suit the purpose, for it lacks a sense of place; pride was in the fact of the city rather than the individual town, it makes no difference whether it is Liskeard or Leeds.

The same problem, the same lack of a sense of place, affects the term 'civic duty'; the impression is of an obligation to society, on a local basis, to promote, say, sanitation and 'useful knowledge', but the emphasis is on the fact of local scale rather than the individual locale; a middle class version of *noblesse oblige*. This chapter is concerned with a sense of civic pride that had Truro as its specific object. A further difficulty arises; if our ideas of civic pride in the early nineteenth century are bound up with the construction of town halls and the development of sanitation schemes then the vessels of that civic pride are necessarily going to be middle class. Does this mean that civic pride is a middle class sentiment or are there ways in which the working classes demonstrated civic pride?

Rosemary Sweet refers to civic pride when discussing electoral politics of the late eighteenth/early nineteenth centuries, suggesting that demonstrations of such local patriotism had a significant impact upon polling and that parliamentary borough elections cannot be properly understood without an appreciation of civic pride.[3] Such is the route by which I came upon this topic, although it was not the use of civic pride for electoral advantage in Truro that was most striking, but the fact that bitter political rivals appeared to be willing to put their differences to one side for the sake of civic pride. Sweet suggests that the desire for parliamentary status was as much a matter of pride as of any practical gain. Frank O'Gorman makes a similar point with reference to Stockton, describing the 'enormous sense of civic excitement' when the town was enfranchised in 1868.[4] In Truro, however, in 1830, local radicals were apparently content to see the town lose one or both of its representatives under the Reform Act, and it was only the actions of one of Lord Falmouth's despised nominees that rescued full parliamentary status for the borough. Most Cornish boroughs, of course, lost their parliamentary status but this seems to have been welcomed by the majority of inhabitants, suggesting that political principle overrode local pride.[5]

Perhaps the best known examples of civic pride are the West Yorkshire woollen towns, with their competitive town hall construction. Bradford's massive new town hall was seen by the leading lights of Leeds as a challenge and the champions of retrenchment abandoned all idea of financial restraint in order to re-establish Leeds' prominent position as not only the pre-eminent town in West Yorkshire but visibly so. Other towns in the area followed suit in attempting to express their sense of local pride through bricks and mortar. This Yorkshire 'town hall mania' occurred in the 1850s, but Manchester and Birmingham had constructed edifices to civic pride twenty years or so before.

Truro too had a new town hall in the middle of the century, officially opened with a grand ceremony on 5 November 1847. There were, of course, numerous speeches extolling the virtues of both town and hall, although the public dinner was held in the Green Market as the new building didn't have a room large enough.[6] So is this an example of civic pride on the West Yorkshire model? In their report on the revised plans for the hall, in August 1845, the *West Briton* suggested that 'the building will probably take precedence of all others of the description in the county'. There is, however, little to suggest that this was the motivation that lay behind the decision to build the hall. Penzance, it is true, had laid the foundation stone of their new Guildhall and Market Hall in July 1836, but this was more than six years before Truro even started planning theirs, and the planning process included no mention of rivals. The title by which the hall is referred to may cast some light. The expressions 'town hall' and 'new hall' were used as a kind of shorthand. On official occasions such as the laying of the foundation stone the building was referred to as the New Law Courts and Market House. These functions not only provided its name but also its *raison d'être*. Rather than any notions of a monument to the glory that was Truro, the prime motivation appears to have been commercial – more market space was needed; this was not only of benefit to the trade of the town but also to the council coffers, as they derived a considerable income from the letting of space in the market. The legal functions of the Municipal Buildings also required more room, especially as the Vice-Warden's Stannary Court had taken to sharing the premises in the early 1840s. There does appear to have been some desire to produce an imposing edifice, but functionalism won out over cost; the tower was scaled down to the modest item to be seen to this day, and the galvanised iron originally intended for the roof was replaced by the cheaper Delabole slate.[7]

In addition to its legal and commercial functions the new hall was, of course, the meeting place for the Town Council. Before the 1835 Municipal Corporations Act the Corporation had been entirely self-elected, and heavily influenced by the patron of the borough, Lord Falmouth, though, it did, on occasion, assert its independence. The struggles between the Corporation and the inhabitants, including various court cases over the legitimacy of harbour dues, led to the municipal body tending to keep its head down rather than displaying civic pride, as all expenditure was greeted with outrage by the reformers. Accusations of financial mismanagement were the keystone of the reformers' campaign against the Corporation, with claims of waste and corruption involving the alienation of Corporate property and the misuse of charitable funds. The large debts of the Corporation had resulted in the appointment of a special committee in 1829 but until then no proper accounts had been kept. It is, therefore, understandable that in the later years of the old Corporation's existence there was an anxiety to avoid conspicuous expenditure that might fuel accusations of profligacy, with reduction of debt carrying more weight than civic symbolism. Even after the 1835 Act the new Council was more concerned with the mundane than with notions of pride; large sums were expended on clearing and widening the channel of the river, and also on the infrastructure of the harbour, but the motivation for this was commerce rather than pride. Briggs suggests that many of the country's new councillors, created by the Muncipal Corporations Act, had a 'narrow civic sense' and points to the fact that civic improvement was still often carried out by Improvement Commissioners rather than the new councils themselves.[8]

In Truro many of the more active Improvement Commissioners were also town councillors, so the difference was merely one of 'hats'. Truro had gained a Paving and Lighting Act in the eighteenth century, the only town in Cornwall to do so, and had acquired a new Act in 1835, just before the Municipal Corporations Act was passed.

Truro City Hall, built in 1847 (Photograph by Anna Tonkin)

Truro's new Improvement Act had been gained by a coalition of all strands of political thought in the town, despite the fact that these differing factions had been at daggers drawn over municipal reform. The first meeting under the new Act, on 15 September 1835, was attended by 76 men, all of whom became Commissioners, though many of them seldom or never attended further meetings. The support was partly financial, as the Commission had the right to levy a rate.[9]

Support for the Improvement Commission in Truro, and for the temporary Board of Health established in 1831, may be considered the best examples of civic pride in the town in the early nineteenth century. While there is certainly an element of self-interest involved, both commercial and personal (the Board of Health was set up to counter the anticipated cholera outbreak in the country), the provision of paving, lighting, drainage and clean water was quite simply of benefit to Truro as a whole. Even areas that did not receive such amenities were assisted in cleansing their streets, to a certain extent. In response to a report in the *West Briton* suggesting that many people were asking 'What is the Truro Board of Health about?', the secretary of the Board, E.J. Spry, responded with a letter to the paper, published 11 October 1833, relating that they had collected more than £150 worth of manure, preventing accumulations in the courts and backlets, erected two sluices to clean out the Kenwyn river, built new, and repaired old, sewers, and built 'necessaries' in some of the densely populated courts. 'Brushes for white-washing, and handbarrows for carrying manure to the carts are lent to any poor persons who may apply to the surveyor'. He concludes: 'I think I may refer with some satisfaction to the very clean state of our streets and courts and ask what has the Truro Board of Health left undone?' Civic pride there, it would seem. The original question as to the Board's activities appears to have been inspired not so much by a lack of practical activity but by the fact that the Falmouth Board met daily while that of Truro only weekly; the difference lay in the fact that Falmouth actually had some cases of cholera while Truro did not. Spry's claims regarding the cleanliness of Truro's streets run counter to the impression of the town contained in Edwin Chadwick's *Report on the Sanitary Condition of the Labouring Population of Great Britain* (1842). However, the section on Truro, written by Charles Barham, appears to have drawn heavily on an account produced in 1824, before the Truro Board of Health's existence, by Dr Clement Carlyon. In this work he refers to 'dirty, ill-ventilated alleys and backlets' and suggests that tenements then being built had courtlets 'so miserably narrow and ill-contrived, that it is hardly possible for them to be kept in a cleanly state'. Carlyon's solution is by means of 'an intelligent and active police', but he recognises that concerted action would be difficult to achieve owing to the variety of interests involved.[10] The Board of Health and the 1835 Improvement Commission could be considered as attempts to co-ordinate action and to provide that 'intelligent and active police'.

Even on this issue, however, the motivation may be considered debatable. Carlyon was certainly very much a Truro man and was no doubt concerned for the well-being of his town – twice mayor of Truro before the 1835 Act and again afterwards, he was one of only four of the last Corporation to be elected to the first Town Council after the Act (eight of the Corporators had stood in the election). He was closely associated with the construction of the Town Hall in 1847 and a bust of him was commissioned for the new building. So Clement Carlyon could, perhaps, be considered Truro's equivalent of Titus Salt, a champion of civic pride, albeit with a professional rather than an industrial background. Salt, created a baronet in 1869, is most associated with Saltaire, the model village he created around his mill in the 1850s. He was also, however, closely associated with Bradford, had mills in the town, was mayor and later, briefly, its MP. Upon his death in 1876 the town afforded him a public funeral. But do Carlyon's activities provide examples of utilitarianism rather than civic pride? It might, of course, seem strange to link Carlyon, the founding president of the Truro Protestant Conservative Association with such a resoundingly liberal philosophy as utilitarianism. The notion, often attributed to Jeremy Bentham, of the greatest happiness for the greatest number of people, was frequently behind measures of sanitation and slum clearance even when these rode roughshod over individual rights, including property rights. Although there were officially 120 Improvement Commissioners, few of them were actively involved and under both the new Act and the old, meetings were usually attended by fifteen members or less, although the first meeting under the new Act attracted a high turnout. The most assiduous attendees of the Improvement Commissioners' meetings were often tradesmen of one description or another. Of the fourteen Committee members preparing the new Improvement Act in 1834, four belonged to the legal profession and six were tradesmen. While it is clearly sensible for the well-being of the town that the busy streets in the commercial area were paved and 'Macadamised' first there is also more than a hint of vested interest involved. Another decision made by the Paving and Lighting Commission in 1834 included extending the 'Kerb' from Fairmantle Street into Tabernacle Street, 'Mr Wm. Hodge the proprietor having consented to pay half the cost'. Mr Wm. Hodge was a member of the Commission and attended the meeting in question.[11]

Concerned commentators like Clement Carlyon and Charles Barham were highly critical of areas like Goodwives Lane, off the top end of Pydar Street, but as the occupants of such areas were too poor to pay their rates they were ineligible to become Improvement Commissioners, or to vote in the post-1835 council elections under the ratepayer franchise, so their homes were the last to receive sanitation, lighting or pavements. In passing it may be noted that the situation in Goodwives Lane bears out the suggestion made by E.P. Thompson that in the great cities the worst landlords were publicans or small shopkeepers that owned just one or two houses to rent out, as a sideline. What was true of the 'great cities' was also true of Truro.[12] Improvement Commissions and Boards of Health were not required by law but were sanctioned by Acts of Parliament. They were augmented in their efforts to improve the physical and moral wellbeing of the town by various charitable organisations: these included a Library, a Humane Association (to assist the needy), a Teetotallers Society, a Horticultural Society, a Bible Society, the Truro Debating Society (later the Truro Institution) and a Geological Society. Many of these were simply branches of national organisations and all of them display slightly sinister signs of being concerned not so much with improvements to the town as with making moral demands of those that they assisted. This included the Truro Lying-In Dispensary that helped 'necessitous married women'.[13] Similarly, the Cornwall Agricultural Association awarded a prize of £5 to 'The Cottager in Kenwyn, Kea, St Clement, Merther or Probus, who shall have brought up the largest family, with the smallest means, and in the best manner without parish relief'. In 1833 the prize went to James Dunstan of Kea who had raised 14 children – £5 was equal to the prize awarded for the best bull and £3 more than that received by the 'best Milch Cow or Heifer'. The Truro supporters of 'the Society for the better observance of the Sabbath could correct the injurious effects produced upon the morals of the lower orders of society by the easy access, they could at all times obtain to beershops etc'.[14] The formation and operation of such associations would appear to owe more to a sense of civic duty than of civic pride.

A different motivation may be discerned in the honouring of those who contributed to the well-being of the town. In 1833 Robert Glasson, landlord of the 'Seven Stars', was presented with 'plate' in recognition of his efforts in establishing the monthly cattle market in Truro. Such presentations were unofficial and partial; not all 'the great and

the good' of the town appreciated the cattle market and there were frequent attempts to get the 'nuisance' moved away from High Cross. The Radical and Tory candidates were also presented with plate after the 1832 election, by their supporters, in recognition of their supposed services to the town.[15] While the latter two examples may owe more to national politics than local pride, that of Glasson was at least a response to material contribution to the town, albeit one of appeal only to certain sections of it.

More permanent, perhaps, and certainly more public, was the honouring of 'local boy' Richard Lander. While not a civic institution, Lander's elevation to the top of a phallic symbol in Lemon Street could be considered an example of local pride in his expeditions to West Africa. In fact, the monument appears to have been something of an accident. If newspaper reports of Lander's activities can be taken as evidence to the degree of interest in his home town and county then the response was distinctly lukewarm, though the *Royal Cornwall Gazette* did carry a report from the expedition the week before Richard Lander died. In fairness, this press silence was as much due to a lack of information as to a lack of interest. Lander's last expedition was an entirely commercial affair and information was a valuable commodity. A book on the subject written in 1835 says, 'We know that he was bound in honour not to send public intelligence, except to the owners of the vessels employed'.[16] Despite this lack of public awareness, Truro did decide to honour him and a subscription was opened to make the customary presentation of plate. Over £80 had been raised when news was received of his death. Unable to make the presentation, the committee decided to erect a monument, but it is clear that this was not the original intention when the subscription was raised, nor therefore was there any intention to elevate Lander above all his fellow townsfolk. Pride there may have been in his achievements, but no more than in the establishment of a monthly cattle market.

Truro's Lander Monument (Photograph by Anna Tonkin)

Lander's is the only secular public monument to a local hero, other than the Admiral Boscawen pub, reflecting not so much a dearth of local talent as a reluctance to place them on pedestals. A contemporary of Lander was Lieutenant General Sir Richard Hussey Vivian, first Baron Vivian. He was one of Wellington's commanders at Waterloo, Whig MP for the Tory Lord Falmouth's pocket borough of Truro, later MP for the King's pocket borough of Windsor, post-reform MP for Truro and later for East Cornwall, a relatively liberal commander of the British army in Ireland and an 'Establishment' figure. Truro did not raise a statue to him, although he was generally afforded respect in the town, despite drawing the wrath of the Tory *Royal Cornwall Gazette*, which claimed not to be angered by his Whiggery but by the inconsistency of which it accused him.[17] Pride by association did not extend to granting pride of place, a by-product, perhaps, of the anti-aristocratic feeling of many of the merchants, bankers and shopkeepers who dominated the counsels, and councils, of the town.

Although they did not put up a statue to him, Hussey Vivian's status as a son of Truro was used to his advantage in the 1832 parliamentary election: the Radical candidate, William Tooke, was a Londoner. In the pre-reform election of 1830 Tooke's campaign had made great efforts to harness not pride in Truro, but in Cornwall. Adverts in the local press made appeals to the Inhabitants 'as Cornishmen, as Englishmen and Britons, as Free and Independent Burgesses of this Loyal, Ancient and highly Respectable Borough'. The words 'Cornishmen' and 'One and All' were used repeatedly, suggesting that the committee organising Tooke's campaign believed there to be a 'Cornish pride' to be tapped.[18] That pride might have been more of a threat than a source of support had those Cornishmen been aware of Tooke's comment, in a letter to Lord Brougham, that he had turned down the safe Radical seat of Finsbury and Holborn because he had 'accidentally become so attached to the Men of Truro … Moreover a respectable constituency of 500 at three hundred miles distance is preferable to 10 000 tag rag and bobtail at my own door'.[19]

It is a notable feature of the 1830s parliamentary reform affair in Cornwall that national politics appears to have carried more weight than local concerns, at least for the leaders of the movement. Reform seems to have been popular in Cornwall despite the fact that the county had more to lose than most other areas. In 1830 Cornwall had 42 MPs (it had been 44 before Grampound's disenfranchisement for corruption); after the 1832 Act this figure had been reduced to just 13. That Truro retained its representation appears to have been, in part at least, due to the efforts of the sitting MPs, nominees of Lord Falmouth, at the time of the passage of the Reform Bill.[20] Due to confusion between the population of the borough and of the town Truro was originally to have lost one of its members. In 1830, however, there was a risk that the town would have lost both members when the validity of its charter was called into question. The question was posed by Truro's own reformers, in a petition against the result of the 'mock election' referred to above. The suggestion made by the Tory *Royal Cornwall Gazette* was that the reformers were willing to sacrifice local interests for the sake of their nationally-based ideology. The *West Briton* printed a denial that Tooke had argued against Truro's right to representation but the *Gazette* countered with quotes from Tooke's counsel and appears to have had the better of that particular argument. Indeed, in March 1831 the *Briton* itself published an account of the election committee hearing in which it says that Mr Adam, Tooke's counsel, 'raised another point on the absolute nullity of the charter of Elizabeth'.[21]

That Cornish supporters of the reform movement in the 1830s treated the reduction of Cornwall's influence at Westminster as a cause for celebration does indeed suggest that national or ideological concerns carried greater weight than local issues and traditions. It may of course be that many of them felt that the influence gained by the Cornish borough seats benefited individuals – often outsiders – rather than the local populace and that they would therefore be better served by a more representative House of Commons. But in the case of Truro the patron was Lord Falmouth who derived much of his income from metallurgical mining and if Truro lost one or both of its seats then the Cornish mining industry risked a serious loss of influence. Although few of Truro's residents were directly involved in the extraction of minerals from the ground, as a Stannary town and a port the industry was of importance, and the bankers who were so influential amongst the town's reformers also relied heavily upon the industry. It could be considered admirable that Truro's reformers were willing to put principle ahead of their personal interests but it also suggests that they put national politics ahead of Truro's position in the scheme of things.

The appeals to Cornish pride in the 1830 election appear to have been targeted at a specific electorate – they were not in common use and were not used to appeal to the freeholders in the county constituency. This suggests a cynical attempt to exploit a sentiment that the self-appointed leading citizens of Truro perceived amongst their lesser brethren. In 1830 Truro was a Corporation Borough, the right to vote being vested only in the 24 members of the Corporation. The reformers, however, were attempting to claim the existence of a ratepayer franchise in the town, under the Elizabethan charter, and were urging all 'Inhabitant Householders' to assert their right to vote. If, as the above appears to suggest, Cornish pride was believed to exist amongst those outside of the professional class and civic institutions in Truro, so too, perhaps, might civic pride in the sense of pride in one's town of residence and/or birth. While the construction of the town hall apparently demonstrated no inter-town rivalry along West Yorkshire lines, the following letter to the *West Briton* in July 1835 suggests otherwise:

> Sir,
>
> I would beg through the medium of your paper, to enquire if there are difficulties which could not be easily surmounted to illuminating our Town Clock with gas? The church of St Mary's is already lit with that excellent light and the extra expense in carrying the very useful, as well as ornamental object into effect, would not now, I presume, be very great! Why then should the inhabitants of the metropolis of the West be still kept in darkness, whilst the little town of Redruth has long since enjoyed the privilege of knowing by their clock, the particular time at any hour of the night as well as by day!
>
> I am, Sir,
>
> Your obedient servant
>
> AN INHABITANT

> P.S. I understand steps are being taken to have illuminative dials at St Austell – Truro surely ought not to be outdone by its neighbours?[22]

Hardly conclusive proof, it is true, but the main argument in support of the point is a fear of Truro being 'outdone by its neighbours'. A further interesting aspect is that the letter is signed 'An Inhabitant' – the form used by supporters of Parliamentary and Municipal reform, being a shortened version of 'Inhabitant Householder' or ratepayer. Without knowing the identity of the letter's author it is impossible to use even this single example to highlight attitudes of any section or class of residents in Truro. But the appeal to pride against neighbouring towns is based entirely on emotion and may be contrasted with the cold rationality exercised by civic leaders. In 1833 there were moves to have the Assize Courts moved from Launceston to Truro. The arguments wheeled out in favour of the move were concerned not with what a wonderful thriving place Truro was, but with its position equidistant between Lands End and Launceston, and the fact that the West Cornwall Parliamentary Division had a greater population than the East, although the petition did include the claim that 'Truro is the chief town of the County'.[23] The campaign is of interest for the way that, as with the Improvement Commission, political foes united for the promotion of Truro, although the committee certainly contained more Reformers than Tories. A further point of interest lies in a comparison of this tendency by Truronians to unite for the benefit of their town with the situation in Bolton, as outlined by Peter Taylor in *Popular Politics in Early Industrial Britain*. There, he suggests, civic leaders divided along strict party lines and whichever party held power at a given time proposed civic improvements and the opposition opposed; if power changed sides, so did opposition.[24]

If civic pride, in the sense of an emotional attachment to one's hometown existed it was not amongst the self-appointed leading citizens. It must be emphasised that by 'self-appointed' reference is intended not only to pre-Municipal Reform members of the Corporation but also the organisers of the reform movement. Such leaders did not emerge from the mass of the populace but from a narrow 'respectable' strata, and any suggestion that waged labourers might have a role to play was treated with not only scorn but downright anger. At a County reform meeting in Bodmin in 1831 a labourer apparently attempted to address the meeting and was laughed at, according to the account in the *Royal Cornwall Gazette*.[25] At a meeting of the Truro Reform Association in 1836 a Tory infiltrator suggested a labourer for the committee and was threatened with violence if he did not apologise for the insult he had offered to the assembled company.[26] So far as civic pride was exhibited by these leading citizens it was in the form of civic duty, the carrying out of which confirmed their status as leading citizens. When not pure self-aggrandisement a commercial edge would generally be found. The building of the new Market Hall and the attempt to gain the Assizes belong to the latter category; the foundation of the various societies and institutes to the former. The activities of the Improvement Commissions contain elements of both motivations while also being, perhaps, the clearest example of civic pride to be found amongst Truro's civic institutions.

It would appear, then, that Truro lacked a sense of the civic pride that the towns of West Yorkshire demonstrated with their town halls, public parks and statues; why

Truro Cathedral was to become the focus of a new civic pride from the late nineteenth century onwards (Photograph by Anna Tonkin)

should this be so? In part, of course, the difference may lie in a misreading of the situation in Yorkshire; perhaps all those civic symbols are a mere façade and no more civic pride existed there than in Truro. Certainly the way that the public recreational spaces were named after their benefactors could be construed as saying more about the personal pride of those benefactors then about the existence of pride in the towns. But even that demonstrates a desire on the part of the locally wealthy to have their name associated with their town in perpetuity. No such pride is evident amongst Truro's residents. In 1845 W.H. Bullmore, a surgeon and supporter of the reform movement, delivered a couple of lectures on the state of Truro's health and the need for recreational space for the inhabitants but he was addressing the subject as one of civic need rather than civic pride.[27]

In attempting to assess the level of civic pride there is a problem in the fact that the judgement is based upon the behaviour of a very small percentage of the population of these towns. We cannot be certain how those who could not afford to endow schools and parks felt about their home towns (in fairness, Bullmore would be in this category). By the end of the nineteenth century working-class support of local sporting teams created the impression of a strong sense of local pride, but earlier in the century no such outlets existed. Here again, however, Cornwall differs from areas such as West Yorkshire as professional sport did not establish itself to the same degree, although sport was played with enthusiasm. In this instance the difference is likely to have a socio-economic explanation; professional sport developed in Britain at a time when Cornwall's population was falling on account of the emigration following the slump in mining. As examples of sport representing local pride one could cite the participation by Cornishmen in hurling matches but these were often intra-town affairs, between married men and single, for example. Alternatively hurling matches might be between town and country in a given neighbourhood; Truro's men would often compete against those of Kenwyn and Kea, the affair frequently ending in a brawl. The continued existence of events such as 'Obby 'Oss in Padstow and Furry Day in Helston in the face of religious and 'rational' attempts at abolition may suggest an element of local pride in the determination of the people to retain their own festivities, but no similar event existed in Truro in the early nineteenth century. There were annual fairs, including one at Whitsun that was later to face calls for its abolition due to the drunkenness and crime that it apparently encouraged and it is perhaps possible that the commonality of Truro took a possessive stance towards that event.[28]

References to class do, of course, raise problems of definition. By suggesting that civic leaders were 'middle class' no account is taken for the wide variations in wealth and status that may be contained within that expression. In the early nineteenth century Truro had an active 'shopocracy' that played an active role in support of the various religious, social and political reform campaigns of the time. It is notable, however, that in the first post municipal reform election in Truro not one of the Reform candidates for the new council was a shopkeeper or publican. One, the Quaker Samuel Milford, was a retired draper. The remainder were bankers like Humphrey Willyams and Edmund Turner, 'merchants' such as John Paddon and John Baynard (there is a clear distinction made between 'merchant' and 'shopkeeper') or medical men like Richard Taunton and

E.J. Spry. Many of these men had been educated outside Cornwall and had connections to professional and political figures in London and elsewhere. After serving as the first post-municipal reform Mayor of Truro, Turner was elected as an MP for the town in 1837. Following his death his place was taken by Willyams. It is possible to detect, to a certain extent, a difference in attitude to civic affairs between the shopkeepers and the 'upper' middle class. On subjects such as slavery there was little difference between them, probably because there was no local element to the issue. With regard to political reform, however, it is the likes of Willyams and Edward Budd, the original editor of the *West Briton*, who appear to have regarded the question in terms of the big picture and who were content to see Truro lose its representation rather than have the old system continue. For the shopocracy, corporate reform appears to have been a bigger issue than that of parliament and the underlying issues had to do with market tolls, quay dues and local commerce in general. One of the two grocers involved in the legal case against the Corporation in 1830, Jeremiah Reynalds, was very involved in the reform movement, acting as a member of the election committee in 1831, but seems to have played little role, if any, in the formation of a Truro branch of the Reform Association. In 1836 he wrote to the new council requesting that they abolish quay dues for Truro Ratepayers, the issue on which he and James Bastian had gone to court and reignited the reform movement in the town. Reynalds' erstwhile partners in reform declined to do so, now that they were responsible for municipal funds. Reynalds' response was to stand for the council himself and he was to serve several terms as Mayor.

This class distinction between the locally-minded, shop-keeping, middle class and the utilitarian adherents of political science, may perhaps contain the reason for the apparent lack of civic pride in Truro. The attitude was that of the civic leaders, drawn from the utilitarian bourgeoisie, not that of the residents in general. Turner, Willyams and Tooke shared a common background with each other and with national figures of utilitarianism such as Bentham and Chadwick. None of them were first generation bourgeoisie. Turner and Willyams were the sons of bankers, Tooke the son of a lawyer. Bentham's father was an attorney, Chadwick's a man of various liberal accomplishments including botany, music and journalism. The Truro shopocracy were generally the offspring of artisans or traders. In Bradford, Titus Salt was the son of a cloth merchant turned farmer. This chapter has been primarily concerned with Truro and is therefore not qualified to assess whether the civic leaders in West Yorkshire, or indeed in other Cornish towns, were less concerned with utilitarian ideals and more rooted in their locale than those of Truro. Nor can confident judgements be made about the degree to which such civic leaders had connections to manual occupations. In seeking explanations for the apparent lack of manifestations of civic pride in Truro in the early nineteenth century I would suggest that the civic leaders looked more to London than to Lemon Street for their inspiration, but that in this they were probably different to their fellow townsmen, possibly deliberately so. Class divisions played a role, although the important class differential was within what we might term the 'middle class' and was a question of education and outlook as much as of vested interest.

Notes

1. Michael Wharton (alias 'Peter Simple'), 'Way of the World' column, *Daily Telegraph*.
2. Briggs, *The Age of Improvement*, London, 1959; A. Briggs, *A Social History of England*, London, 1987.
3. R. Sweet, 'Freemen and Independence in English Borough Politics', *Past and Present*, November 1998.
4. F. O'Gorman, 'Campaign Rituals and Ceremonies', *Past and Present*, May 1992.
5. *Royal Cornwall Gazette*, 31 July 1830.
6. *West Briton*, 15 October 1847.
7. *West Briton*, 12 September 1845.
8. Briggs, *Age of Improvement*, p. 277.
9. Truro Council papers, Cornwall Record Office (CRO hereafter), B/TRU 115/1.
10. CRO, EN/P/425, C. Barham, *Report on the Sanitary State of Truro*, 1840; C. Carlyon, *Observations on the Endemic Typhus Fever of Cornwall*, 1825.
11. CRO, B/TRU 115/1.
12. E.P. Thompson, *The Making of the English Working Class*, London, 1980.
13. H.L. Douch, *The Book of Truro*, Chesham, 1977.
14. *Royal Cornwall Gazette*, 9 March and 4 May 1833.
15. *Royal Cornwall Gazette*, 20 April and 7 September 1833.
16. R. Huish, *The Travels of Richard Lander*, London, 1835.
17. *Royal Cornwall Gazette*, 21 July 1837.
18. *Royal Cornwall Gazette*, 31 July 1830.
19. University College London, Brougham Collection, 10.323.
20. *Royal Cornwall Gazette*, 23 April 1831.
21. *West Briton*, 19 March 1831.
22. *West Briton*, 28 July 1835.
23. *West Briton*, 5 April 1833.
24. Peter Taylor, *Popular Politics in Early Industrial Britain: Bolton 1825-1850,* Keele, 1995, p. 90.
25. *Royal Cornwall Gazette*, c.1831.
26. *West Briton*, 2 October 1836.
27. *Royal Cornwall Gazette*, 28 February 1845.
28. Douch, *Book of Truro*.

'So beautifully Cornish': The Church heritage and identity creation

Graham Busby

Introduction

In a county well-endowed with examples of the built heritage, the Anglican parish church provides a key to cultural practices through the centuries. Even Victorian 'restoration' does not eliminate the sense of antiquity; indeed, for some visitors this pastiche, such as at Blisland, 'restored' by Eden to his interpretation of the colour and brilliance of what existed before the Reformation, is commended by Davidson.[1] In terms of numbers, the 2001 Truro Diocesan Directory refers to 224 churches of which 130 are listed Grade I and 66 are II*, representing 58% and 29% of the total respectively. The importance of the church heritage in the indigenous cultural legacy cannot be over-stated; the church both symbolises Cornish culture, historically, and to some extent reproduces it; in contemporary tourism, the historically layered relations intersect with newer social ones. This chapter considers how the church heritage both influences and, to some extent, cements individual identity. The discussion in this chapter is derived from visitors' book comments from three churches (Gunwalloe, Lanteglos-by-Fowey and St Just-in-Roseland), which, it is argued, provide an insight into visitor motivations and experiences. This form of data is useful because it is generated by the visitor with no researcher influence although a certain level of subjectivity may exist with regard to the interpretation of themes.

Visitors Books and qualitative research

Data from visitors' books is of particular value in attempting to chart an individual's interest in Cornish churches. The visitors' book research adopts content analysis in depth, a method previously employed in relation to heritage visitor attractions by Brice et al.[2] The ontological background to this study, i.e. nature of reality, assumes multiple constructions that are both socially and experientially-based but, as importantly, depend for their content on the individual – a resonance here with Richards who asserts that 'no two individuals can have the same experience'.[3] On the other hand, yet still from a phenomenological perspective, Schutz argues that it is misleading to suggest 'that experiences *have* meaning. Meaning does not lie in the experience. Rather, those experiences are meaningful which are grasped reflectively', a point also emphasised by Giddens and Van Manen.[4]

Interior of Lanteglos church (Postcard from the Mac Waters collection)

The immediate question this raises is the temporal dimension of reflexivity: does the reflection occur two hours after the experience? Straight after it? During it? Regardless of when the reflection occurs, Schutz's view may go a long way to explaining the occurrence of repeat visitors, identified in the visitors' book findings: after reflection, their (first – and subsequent) visit has taken on meaning. In the visitors' books, for all three survey churches, comments sometimes refer to a visit many years before or there are statements such as 'our fourth visit in six years'. It is argued that, this alone, indicates the church has some level of meaning to the individual's identity. Finnegan raises the issue of *audience*: for whom is the visitors' book comment intended?[5] Whilst most of the entries, at all three sites, are neutral, a number imply that it is the church authorities, presumably the church-wardens/parochial church council, who will, hopefully, see that a visitor has appreciated the building being kept open; in this context, the comments are probably 'unconscious decisions'.[6] Only once, in the three visitors' books, does an alternative, distinctive audience emerge, viz. relatives in the congregation or other readers who have genealogical interests: at Lanteglos, on 23 May, a visitor from California states that their grand-father, four generations back, came from the parish and 'anyone by name of Endean please write'. There is, then, a general audience, one for the church authorities, and one for relations or affinity interests.

However, it is also likely that the individual simply wishes to leave a mark. To this end, Fowler views the 'Visitors' Book' as 'a surrogate for such monumental scribbling' as found in the form of ancient graffiti at the St Ninian's Cave Christian shrine in

Scotland.[7] This has more of a resonance with the concept of writer as both producer and consumer; indeed, as Shaw & Williams observe, visitors are not passive, their 'consumption informs production'.[8] Finally, it is noted that research by Brice et al suggested that local residents were unlikely to make an entry whereas international visitors would; perhaps, this is simply indicative of level of *familiarity*, that is, residents see the site frequently, visitors from further afield do not and are, therefore, more likely to want to state they have visited.[9]

Whilst visitors' books were readily available for Gunwalloe and Lanteglos-by-Fowey, for the year 2000, that for St Just-in-Roseland covered the first quarter of the year, the remainder – and that for 2001 – had been mislaid; this did not become apparent until after much analysis had been undertaken with the two books for 2000. For St Just, the 2002 data has been used, given that it covers the full twelve months. A further point to note is that at Lanteglos, after opening on 1 January, the church was closed until mid-April to permit major re-roofing and re-wiring to take place. What, then, do visitors' book comments suggest about the church heritage and identity creation? The genealogical aspect has been alluded to above; this and other influences are now discussed.

Table 1 Geographic distribution of visitors to churches, according to visitors' books

	Gunwalloe		*St Just*		*Lanteglos*	
	2000	*%*	*2002*	*%*	*2000*	*%*
United Kingdom	4882	91	9668	87	824	84
Europe exc. UK	233	4	673	6	84	9
North America	162	3	408	4	42	4
Australia/New Zealand	75	1	249	2	25	3
Africa	17	<1	52	<1	5	<1
Asia	7	<1	24	<1		
South America	3	<1	6	<1	1	<1
Caribbean/Bermuda	3	<1	5	<1		

Research from Cohen, McKercher and Timothy, addressing the relevance of *depth* of experience and *connectivity* with visitor attractions, comes across in a large minority of visitors' book comments.[10] A number of themes found in the visitors' books indicate that the individual sites do have particular meaning for some visitors; in other words, there is a contested heritage. However, despite the prevalence of commodification at a great many heritage sites, the three survey churches exhibit few manifestations (guide leaflets and postcards). Given this, Prentice and Keeling argue that churches attract both the general interest (recreational) visitor and special interest visitor; for the general interest visitor, it is argued that perception of the church can be coloured by wider representations of Cornwall, whereby an element of 'Otherness' resides in the tourist gaze; however, although this is unlikely to be consciously articulated, it may well influence perceptions of identity.[11] Before considering the themes of relevance to identity creation, a review of geographic origins is presented in Table 1, above. The figures presented are conservative; for example, where an entry reads the *Jones Family*, this has been interpreted as three and where only one name is entered, this has been taken to represent a single individual despite the probability of there being at least two visitors, based on personal observation, in 2002, and a substantial face-to-face survey.[12]

Mobility and biography – the search for 'roots'

The theme of returning to one's roots is evident from many of the entries – not surprising given the emigration figures; the 'Cornish diaspora', of the nineteenth century, whereby many thousands emigrated to Australia, New Zealand, the USA, Canada and South Africa,[13] might account for a large proportion of visitors, to the county, from these nations today – it is certainly considered to be an important tourist market – although empirical data is limited.[14] The number of descendants is substantial; Payton, citing Deacon's research, observes that nearly a quarter of a million emigrated between 1840 and 1900 and, in the latter year, around a quarter of the white miners on the South African Rand were Cornish.[15] Reporting another estimate, Payton asserts that, in 1992, there were between 245,000 and 290,000 Australians with a significant level of Cornish descent and, possibly, up to 850,000 with a Cornish connection; he also discusses the strength of identification with Cornwall for descendants living in the United States, Canada and South Africa.[16] Table 1 is illuminating for the emphasis on visitors from North America, Australia and New Zealand.

Numerous entries in the Gunwalloe visitors' book allude to diasporic connections; for example: 'We have ancestors buried here – a special moment', written on 22 April 2000, by a New Zealander. From Lanteglos, on 23 April, examples from Australian and Canadian visitors are presented: a visitor from Victoria, Australia states that he is the 'great-great-great grandson of Thomas Nunn Jewell and Elizabeth. Buried here 1882'. On 10 May, two visitors, from Toronto, Canada, state 'Grandparents' resting place – (Pearce's from Trevecca Farm)'. An entry for 18 May, from an Australian, visitor, queries 'Decendant (sic) of HENRY BATE??? Buried in churchyard'. Similarly, from St Just, examples from four nations are illustrated: on 23 May, 'Here for generations my mother's father's family (Kendell) worshipped' (visitor from Alberta, Canada) and, on 4 October, South Africans write 'We finally found our roots, we're so proud to be Pascoe's' (sic) – in 1903, Johannesburg was 'but a suburb of Cornwall'.[17] On 22 October, visitors from California, state 'Church of our ancestors' and, on 26 December, a New Zealand family writes 'Tracing our ancestor Eleanor Wolgrove': the time of year does not deter this visitor type. A domestic tourist (Surrey), rather than one from a diasporic destination, notes at St Just, on 15 February, that he is a 'Relative of John Luer 1542 (Vicar)' – the only ecclesiastical roots connection stated in the visitors' books.

Such visitors can be perceived as conforming to Cohen's *existential mode*, those who desire 'to find one's spiritual roots. The visit takes on the quality of a home-coming to a historical home'.[18] This is echoed by McCain & Ray in their paper on legacy tourists, as they term them, whereby such visitors might garner a 'feeling of completeness'.[19] This typifies Ryan's observations that the activity can be both expressive and instrumental: self-expression and affiliative needs combine with religious-philosophical ones to produce a sense of achievement once the site is reached.[20] On the other side of the world, Lew and Wong have observed the same phenomenon, also through the use of content analysis.[21] The motivation for these visitors is clear: a search for fine details of their background, to a narrative of self.

Additionally, it is argued that Pearce's discussion is relevant, that is, both cognitive-normative and interactional forms can be discerned within the same visitor: cognitive-normative refers to the motivation, viz. a search for roots, plus there is an interaction between the visitor and the site – for example, gravestones may be sought, resulting in a higher quality of experience highlighting McKercher's *depth* of experience axis.[22] From another perspective, Gruffudd et al have observed that visitors locate their 'roots' through visits partly because of the technological bases of modern lifestyles.[23] Technology has changed lifestyles for many in the last six decades, including Normandy veterans; it is argued that the St Just visitor, from Oxfordshire, on 5 September, was involved with the D-Day Landings (many troops being stationed in the area): 'To re-trace my granddads steps in World War 2'. Roots of a non-genealogical type, as also applies to a woman from Lancashire, who simply stated on 25 September: 'Late Trevernal Camp ATS 43/44' (St Just). Without doubt, both genealogical and non-genealogical roots visitors illustrate Pearce's self-directed Travel Career component whereby a specific motivation is being fulfilled.[24] Intriguingly, comments from the Lanteglos data indicate only genealogical roots visitors there.

Another feature of the data is that visitors from the two Commonwealth countries of Australia and Canada are spread fairly evenly through the year; statistically insignificant but worthy of further research for tourist board purposes. If the year 2000 figures, for overseas visitors, are compared to the Cornwall Holiday Survey (hereafter, CHS) for 1999, the differences may well be explained by familial connections with Gunwalloe.[25] For example, the Holiday Survey suggests that 1.0% of respondents (n=4,416) were from North America; the Gunwalloe figures indicate that 3.0% were from the USA and Canada, for St Just it is 3.7% and 4.3% for Lanteglos. Similarly, hidden with the CHS 'Elsewhere' category, i.e. overseas apart from North America and Europe, are Australia, New Zealand and South Africa: all key nations in terms of the Cornish diaspora.[26] Respondents from 'elsewhere' in the CHS 1999 data represent 0.7% of the total; for Gunwalloe this is 1.95%, or for Australia, New Zealand and South Africa, alone, 1.7%; the same three nations represent 2.6% at St Just and 3% at Lanteglos. Consideration of these figures emphasises Hale's argument that roots tourism is an important market and, perhaps, as Lowenthal observes, 'humble origins are newly chic'.[27]

'The romantic gaze' and biography

The tourist discourse articulates notions of 'romantic Cornwall' with places and topographical features: it is argued that the Cornish church figures prominently although not to the same extent as deserted mine engine houses, castles and cliffs. A number of comments appear to justify the church as being the object of the romantic, historic gaze for many visitors: 'A glorious sight. Windows are lovely and ceiling beams the best

Gunwalloe church (Photograph by Sarah Chapman)

we've seen.[28] Well carved' (22 April, Gunwalloe); 'First visit here, wildly romantic' (23 April, Gunwalloe); 'Jane —— a lover of old churches' (4 May, Gunwalloe); 'What a glorious heritage we have' (12 September, Gunwalloe); and from a German visitor 'First time here and I'm surprised to see a church in this unusual rough and windy spot. I think in former times 11th/12th century when life was difficult for these poor people here, they were in urgent need of a church and the help of a mighty power – perhaps God?' (15 September, Gunwalloe). At Lanteglos, on 19 November, a visitor writes: 'Romance and dreams have a home here'. Nearly a third of comments at Gunwalloe suggest aesthetic satisfaction whilst the figures rise to 50% at St Just and 55% at Lanteglos.

The three survey churches do not have a monopoly on high quality scenery or atmosphere since these are features present in many (most?) of the Cornish church settings. Indeed, the CHS for 1999 identified scenery and atmosphere as being significant attractions for visitors to the county, comprising 21.5% and 6.2% of responses to the 'most important reason for choosing Cornwall'.[29] Therefore, on the basis of Prentice's categorization of heritage attractions, these comments illustrate the juxtaposition of 'countryside' or 'seascape' with 'religious attraction' whereby the sum of the parts is greater than any individual element.[30] Aesthetic satisfaction is illustrated by these comments and by those with a little more brevity such as 'Beautiful church in a pretty location' (30 May, Gunwalloe) and 'An elegant church' (29 April, Lanteglos). Whilst accepting that aesthetic satisfaction runs close to notions of spirituality,[31] it is argued that comments can be differentiated – some will comprise both aesthetic and spiritual observations, one possibly influencing the other; a good example, provided by a visitor, is illustrated thus: 'Uplifting both spiritually and aesthetically' (16 February, St Just).

The overall impression gained from many of the entries conforms to Tresidder's observation that 'sacred spaces act as a means of reference, their association with nostalgia, heritage, community or the natural, allow us to find roots in a rootless world' – a theme echoed by Digance, Shackley and Wang.[32] Whilst many visitors are deliberately seeking to recapture these associations, for others the church is an unexpected find: 'Such a lovely place, didn't know places like this existed' (2 July, from Manchester re Gunwalloe) and 'What a beautiful church you have! It is nice to stumble upon a true Cornish treasure. It is a place of true beauty and thank you for keeping the doors open so that we could come in and share it!' (18 March, Gunwalloe). For these visitors, the past is recreated in an idealised way;[33] prior knowledge is not indicated by the comments, interaction with the site very much is. Interaction with the site is demonstrated, palpably, by visitors familiar with Daphne du Maurier's oeuvre; given the du Maurier connection with Lanteglos (she was married there on 19 July 1932), it is not surprising to find five references spread throughout the year; two typical entries are: 'Can see where Daphne du Maurier gained some of her inspiration' (visitor from Ruthin, Wales, 26 April) and 'Felt Daphne's spirit' (German visitor, 8 July). The nationality of the latter author highlights the global-local nexus of *du Maurier Country*.

An example of prior knowledge of one of the sites and interaction is provided by the following entry from 11 August 2000 at Gunwalloe:

> Rita and Bob —— came here following in the footsteps of George Kemp who was G. Marconi's right hand man. Kemp visited this church most Sundays whilst he was supervising the errection (sic) of Marconi's aerial and transmitter for the Atlantic leap by wireless telegraph. Marconi received the letter 'S' (three dots) at Signal Hill, Newfoundland on Dec 12 1901 which was transmitted from the site adjacent to the Poldhu Hotel on the furthest side of next bay. God helped him with this work which provided the foundation for todays communications.

Such comments illustrate the temporal and secular link between church and landscape – and it is argued individual biography and, thus, personal identity. Landscape and the *gaze* are also encapsulated by specific comments concerning the natural environment – at Gunwalloe, the sea might be spectacular or protection is offered from the wind and rain. The words sea, waves and wind are referred to in 44, 8 and 19 entries, respectively, whereas landscape appreciation is expressed in terms such as *beautiful setting*, *surroundings* or *location*; these occur 6, 14 and 3 times. These comments reflect Betjeman, Brabbs, Davidson, Hammond, Henderson, Jenkins, Mee, Moncrieff and Salmon, in their guide book descriptions besides having a resonance with Schama's observations on landscape and memory.[34]

The setting at St Just-in-Roseland is, arguably, world famous; some visitors perceive the graveyard as gardens, typified by comments such as 'A secret garden' (24 May) and 'Wonderful gardens' (18 June), some suggest it is 'Better than Helligan' (sic) (6 August) and 'Better than the Eden Project' (24 October). Commentators at St Just refer to guide book authors: 'J. Betjemann (sic) was right, true words' (1 May), 'Betjeman was right' (22 September) and 'We came because of H.V. Morton's book of 1928 and it's still as lovely as described' (27 August). Presumably, the latter is his *In Search of England*.[35] It is

St Just-in-Roseland church (Postcard from Mac Waters Collection)

not surprising, therefore, that just over 10% of comments at St Just address the surrounding environment. The juxtaposition of these churches in such settings would appear to improve the *experience*, one that it is up to each individual visitor to interpret. A combination of commentary on the weather and usage of a specific guide book is indicated by a comment for 19 April 2000 (Gunwalloe): 'Just as Simon Jenkins describes on this foul day', referring to his *England's Thousand Best Churches*.[36] A County Durham visitor at Lanteglos, on 6 June, states 'Following 'England's 1000 Best Churches. The book is right, it's very hard to find!' – sequestered as it is above a side creek of the River Fowey between hills.

The topography may have been the motivation to visit, after all, there is no admission charge unlike Heligan or The Eden Project, when St Just is considered, and thus the cognitive-normative form of visitor can be discerned. However, it is considered that the interactional form is likely to predominate: visitors walking the extensive grounds experience surprise at the range of sub-tropical flora. As an adjunct to this motivation, none of the roots-based visitors make any references, despite Stephenson's assertion that landscapes have a positive effect on diasporic groups[37] – probably, the thoughts of these visitors are, first and foremost, on their ancestral connections.

The 'Otherness' – Celticity dimension

Table 2, overleaf, indicates the large number of sites associated with Celtic saints in Cornwall; for visitors unaware of this 'classification', the names serve to reinforce a perception of 'otherness' – a point also emphasised by Harvey.[38] Expressions, for Gunwalloe, dedicated to St Winwalloe, such as 'queer little church by the sea' (3 January) and 'we don't get churches like this at home' (1 February, visitor from Melbourne, Australia) imply that the church might be 'different-looking from those of other counties' as Canon Miles Brown believes visitors are likely to think.[39] Added to this is the fact that 68 entries refer to it being a *little* church; clearly, these visitors are used to rather larger properties. However, four entries refer, specifically, to St Winwalloe – another of the aspects that Brown considers might puzzle visitors. Orme's research concerning these Celtic *saints* is for the serious student of Cornish studies rather than the average visitor[40] – although it is hard to avoid noticing their names on road signs and dedication boards at church entrances, themselves. One of the themes to emerge from a study of these *saints* is their harmony with the environment and a lack of grandeur. This has a relationship with words and comments concerning the simplicity of the place, in a busy modern world: resonances with John Lowerson's comment that 'Cornwall has come almost to represent a British Tibet; distant, valued by outsiders and threatened by an occupying power'.[41]

Table 2: Church and chapel sites of 'Celtic' saints in Cornwall

Total number of saints venerated at sites in Cornwall		140
Relationship of saints to sites:	Saints with 1 site	112
	2 sites	18
	3 sites	3
	4 sites	3
	5 sites	1
	6 sites	1
	8 sites	1
Approximate number of saints unique to Cornwall		78[42]

At St Just, a visitor from Gosport states 'This glorious Celtic church is beautiful' (9 May), one, from Bristol, simply states 'Pre Augustine!' (10 July), and a Canadian, 'very different' (23 September). However, at Lanteglos, very much an example of a Celtic Christian site within its lan, and incorporating two Cornish nouns, there are no references to Celtic aspects. Indeed, there is little to indicate a perception of 'otherness' apart from 'So beautifully Cornish' (23 December). Reflection on the comment from St Just, on 9 May, above, generates the question as to whether the visitor was viewing the church as Celtic or, because it is in Cornwall, the church as Cornish (Celtic); in other words, the county, as a totality, can be perceived as Celtic and, arguably, for visitors there are more readily-identifiable Celtic sites (example: Chysauster, promoted in English Heritage's promotional literature as Celtic and with reference to the Cornish language). Deacon's observation is very pertinent here: 'within the 'tourist' discourse of Cornwall, the sign "Celtic" becomes a moment attached to "romance", "tradition", "King Arthur", "standing stones", "jewellery" and so on'.[43] In the absence of much (or any) *interpretation*, the visitor is left to construe their own Cornish church *heritage*; cultural construction of Cornwall is argued to influence many in their interpretation of the church. This returns us to the consideration of reflexivity; with space-time compression, Breathnach argues that individuals 'deal with their experience of life in modernity by asserting a relationship with the past in material form. People may use heritage attractions as another way of fulfilling their need for a glacial conception of time. In doing so, people are acting reflexively'.[44]

Conclusion

This chapter has utilised comments from visitors' books at three churches in order to chart individual motivations and experiences. Whilst it is apparent that those seeking 'roots' are, axiomatically, concerned with issues of identity, it is argued that other themes also indicate a search for self, for self-actualisation and, thereby, identity. The individuals with an interest in Marconi's right-hand man manifest characteristics of special-interest tourists and, concurrently, a component of their identity. As Chhabra et al put it, 'strangers get together in a cultural production to share a feeling of closeness and solidarity',[45] something missing for many in contemporary life. This is, arguably, also evident in media portrayals such as the television series *Doc Martin*, based around the fictional Port Wenn (in reality, Port Isaac). In Cornwall, these strangers fall into two categories, those who claim ethnic descent and those who do not – although they may feel some Celtic elective affinity.[46] The data in Table 1 supports the argument for visitors claiming ethnic descent, to some extent, but, preceding lower per unit travel costs,[47] by a decade, it is argued that the flowering of Cornish Associations in America, and other countries, from the 1970s on stimulated the extant interest in Cornish roots for many. On a contemporary level, Alan Kent has documented the relevance of Cornwall to the identity of those in various parts of mainland USA.[48]

Returning to one's roots is a form of heritage tourism, confirming the tourist's identity via a potentially romantic image of their past.[49] Although overall visitor numbers are not high, roots tourism (or genealogical tourism, as Meethan terms it)[50] constitutes an important market which is just one of the beneficiaries of lower per-unit air travel costs. Shaw & Williams posit the question: 'how are tourism structures and flows created?'[51] It is argued that diasporic tourism, catalysed by lower air fares and a search for identity, has created a scape, a flow. Cornwall's churches are, then, an active agent in shaping, or confirming, visitors' identities. Drawing on Johnson's *circuits of culture*, it is argued that this conceptualisation helps to illustrate how visitors construct – or amend – their self-identity in the light of minimal *text*, in Cornish churches, which results in truly phenomenological *readings*.[52] These *readings*, or interpretations, are carried home with concomitant longer-term *impacts*. Whilst it appears *prima facie* that there may be little effect on production, the number and form of texts has developed in the last decade – consider the world-wide web sites which recognises the need to cater for the diasporic visitor. There is also a resonance here with Ashworth's assertion that "you cannot sell *your* heritage to tourists: you can only sell *their* heritage back to them in your locality".[53]

Notes

1. R. Davidson, *Cornwall*, B.T. Batsford, 1978.
2. J. Brice, G. Busby and P. Brunt, 'English Rural Church Tourism: A Visitor Typology', *Acta Turistica*, 2003, Vol. 15, No. 2, pp. 144-162.
3. G. Richards, 'The experience industry and the creation of attractions', in G. Richards (ed.) *Cultural Attractions and European Tourism*, Wallingford, CABI Publishing, 2001, pp. 55-69 (p. 56).
4. A. Schutz, *The Phenomenology of the Social World*, London: Heinemann, 1972, p. 69; A. Giddens, *New Rules of Sociological Method*, 2nd edition, Cambridge: Polity, 1993; M. Van Manen, *Researching lived experience*, State University Press of New York, 1990.
5. R. Finnegan, 'Using documents', in R. Sapsford & V. Jupp (eds.) *Data Collection and Analysis*, Sage, 1996, pp. 138-151.
6. R. Finnegan, 'Using documents', in R. Sapsford & V. Jupp (eds.) *Data Collection and Analysis*, Sage, 1996, pp. 138-151 (p. 144).
7. P.J. Fowler, *The Past in Contemporary Society: Then, Now*, Routledge, 1992, p. 72.
8. G. Shaw and A. Williams, *Tourism and Tourism Spaces*, Sage, 2004, p. 13.
9. J. Brice, G. Busby and P. Brunt, 'English Rural Church Tourism: A Visitor Typology', *Acta Turistica*, 2003, Vol. 15, No. 2, pp. 144-162.
10. E. Cohen, 'A Phenomenology of Tourist Experience', *Sociology*, Vol. 13, 1979, pp. 179-201; B. McKercher, 'Towards a classification of cultural tourists', *International Journal of Tourism Research*, Vol. 4, 2002, No. 1, pp. 29-38; D. Timothy, 'Tourism and the personal heritage experience', *Annals of Tourism Research*, Vol. 23, 1997, No. 4, pp. 948-950.
11. R. Prentice, *Tourism and Heritage Attractions*, Routledge, 1993; Keeling, A., 'Church Tourism – providing a ministry of welcome to visitors', *Insights*, 2000, pp. A13-A22.
12. G. Busby, 'The contested Cornish church heritage', in P. Payton (ed.) *Cornish Studies: Twelve*, Exeter: University of Exeter Press, 2004, pp. 166-183.
13. A.L. Rowse, *The Cornish in America*, Jonathan Cape, 1969; P. Payton, *The Cornish Overseas*, Fowey: Alexander Associates, 1999; A.L. Rowse, *A Cornishman at Oxford*, Jonathan Cape, 1965.
14. A. Hale, 'Representing the Cornish', *Tourist Studies*, Vol. 1, 2001, No. 2, pp. 185-196.
15. Payton, *The Cornish Overseas*.
16. Payton, *The Cornish Overseas*.
17. C.L. Hind, *Days in Cornwall*, 2nd edition, London, 1907, p. 352, cited in P. Payton, *A.L. Rowse and Cornwall*, University of Exeter Press, 2005.
18. E. Cohen, 'A Phenomenology of Tourist Experience', *Sociology*, Vol. 13, pp. 179-201 (p. 191).
19. G. McCain and N.M. Ray, 'Legacy tourism: the search for personal meaning in heritage travel', *Tourism Management*, Vol. 24, No. 6, pp. 713-717 (p. 716).
20. C. Ryan, *Researching Tourist Satisfaction – issues, concepts, problems*, London: Routledge, 1995.
21. A. Lew and A. Wong, 'News from the Motherland: a content analysis of existential tourism magazines in Southern China, Tourism', *Culture and Communication*, Vol. 4, 2003, No. 2, pp. 83-94.
22. P.L. Pearce, *The Ulysses Factor – evaluating visitors in tourist settings*, New York: Springer-Verlag, 1988; B. McKercher, 'Towards a classification of cultural tourists', *International Journal of Tourism Research*, Vol. 4, No. 1, pp. 29-38;
23. P. Gruffudd, D.T. Herbert and A. Piccini, '"Good to think": social constructions of Celtic heritage in Wales', *Environment and Planning D: Society and Space*, Vol. 17, 1999, No. 6, pp. 705-721.
24. P.L. Pearce, *The Ulysses Factor – evaluating visitors in tourist settings*, New York: Springer-Verlag, 1988
25. Tourism Research Group, *Cornwall Holiday Survey 1999,* Exeter: University of Exeter, 1999.
26. A.L. Rowse, *The Cornish in America*, London: Jonathan Cape, 1969; P. Payton, *The Cornish Overseas*, Fowey: Alexander Associates, 1999; A.L. Rowse, *A Cornishman at Oxford*, London: Jonathan Cape, 1965.
27. A. Hale, 'Representing the Cornish', *Tourist Studies*, Vol. 1, No. 2, pp. 185-196; D. Lowenthal, *The heritage crusade and the spoils of history*, London: Viking, 1996, p. 17.
28. J. Urry, 'Gazing on history', in D. Boswell & J. Evans (eds.) *Representing the Nation: A Reader – Histories, Heritage and Museums*, London: Routledge, 1999, pp. 208-232.
29. Tourism Research Group, *Cornwall Holiday Survey 1999,* University of Exeter, 1999, p. 26.
30. R. Prentice, *Tourism and Heritage Attractions*, Routledge, 1993.
31. R. Scruton, *An Intelligent Person's Guide to Modern Culture*, Duckworth, 1998.
32. R. Tresidder, 'Tourism and Sacred Landscapes', in D. Crouch (ed.) *Leisure/Tourism Geographies – practices and geographical knowledge*, Routledge, 1999, pp. 137-148 (p. 144); J. Digance, 'Pilgrimage at contested sites', *Annals of Tourism Research*, Vol. 30, No. 1, pp. 143-159; M. Shackley, 'Space, Sanctity and Service; the English Cathedral as heterotopia', *International Journal of Tourism Research*, Vol. 4, No. 5, pp. 345-352; N. Wang, *Tourism and modernity – a sociological analysis*, Pergamon, 2000.
33. I. Reader, 'Conclusions', in I. Reader and T. Walter (eds.) *Pilgrimage in Popular Culture*, Macmillan, 1993, pp. 220-246.
34. J. Betjeman, *Sir John Betjeman's Guide to English Parish Churches*, Harper Collins, 1958, revised and updated by Nigel Kerr, 1993; D. Brabbs, *English Country Churches*, Weidenfeld & Nicholson, 1985; R. Davidson, *Cornwall*, B.T. Batsford, 1978; R.J.W. Hammond, *West Cornwall and the Isles of Scilly*, 4th edition, Ward Lock, 1966; C. Henderson,

Cornish Church Guide and Parochial History of Cornwall, Truro: D. Bradford Barton, 1925, 1964; S. Jenkins, *England's Thousand Best Churches*, Allen Lane, 1999; A. Mee, *The King's England – Cornwall*, Hodder & Stoughton, 1937; A.R.H. Moncrieff, *Black's Guide to Cornwall*, Adam & Charles Black, 1907; A.L. Salmon, *The Little Guide – Cornwall*, 9th edition, revised by Hicks, R., Methuen & London: Batsford, 1903, 1950; S. Schama, *Landscape and Memory*, Harper Collins1995.

35. H.V. Morton, *In Search of England*, Methuen, 1927.
36. S. Jenkins, *England's Thousand Best Churches*, Allen Lane, 1999;
37. M.L. Stephenson, 'Tourism, racism and the UK Afro-Caribbean diaspora', in T. Coles and D.J. Timothy (eds.) *Tourism, diaspora and space*, Routledge, 2004, pp. 62-77.
38. D.C. Harvey, 'Constructed landscapes and social memory: tales of St Samson in early medieval Cornwall', *Environment and Planning D: Society and Space*, Vol. 20, No. 2, 2002, pp. 231-248.
39. H.M. Brown, *What to look for in Cornish Churches*, David & Charles, 1973, p.9.
40. N. Orme, *English Church Dedications with a Survey of Cornwall and Devon*, University of Exeter, 1996; N. Orme, *The Saints of Cornwall*, Oxford University Press, 2000
41. J. Lowerson, 'Celtic Tourism – some recent magnets', in P. Payton (ed.) *Cornish Studies: Two*, University of Exeter Press, 1994, pp. 128-137 (p. 135).
42 Source adapted from N. Orme, *The Saints of Cornwall*, Oxford University Press, 2000
43. B. Deacon, From '"Cornish Studies" to "Critical Cornish Studies": reflections on methodology', in P. Payton (ed.) *Cornish Studies: Twelve*, University of Exeter Press, 2004, pp. 13-29 (p. 18).
44. T. Breathnach, 'Looking for the real me: locating the self in heritage tourism', *Journal of Heritage Tourism*, Vol. 1, No. 2, 2006, pp. 100-120 (p. 103).
45. D. Chhabra, R. Healy and E. Sills, 'Staged authenticity and heritage tourism', *Annals of Tourism Research*, Vol. 30, No. 5, 2003, pp. 702-719 (p. 705).
46. A. Hale, 'Whose Celtic Cornwall?' in D.C. Harvey, R. Jones, N. McInroy and C. Milligan (eds.) *Celtic Geographies: Old Culture, New Times*, Routledge, 2002, pp. 157-170.
47. T. Coles, D.T. Duval and C.M. Hall, 'Tourism, mobility and global communities: new approaches to theorising tourism and tourist spaces', in W.F. Theobald (ed.) *Global Tourism*, 3rd edition, Amsterdam, Elsevier, 2005, pp. 463-481.
48. A. Kent, *Cousin Jack's Mouth-Organ – Travels in Cornish America*, St Austell: Cornish Hillside Publications, 2004.
49. C. Palmer, 'Tourism and the symbols of identity', *Tourism Management*, Vol. 20, No. 3, 1999, pp. 313-321.
50. K. Meethan, '"To stand in the shoes of my ancestors" – tourism and genealogy', in T. Coles and D.J. Timothy (eds.) *Tourism, diasporas and space*, London: Routledge, 2004, pp. 139-150.
51. G. Shaw and A. Williams, *Tourism and Tourism Spaces*, Sage, 2001, p. 4.
52. R. Johnson, 'The story so far and further transformation', in D. Punter (ed.) *Introduction to contemporary studies*, Harlow, Longman, 1986, pp. 277-313.
53. G.J. Ashworth, *Let's sell our Heritage to Tourists?* London Council for Canadian Studies, cited in G. Evans, 'Mundo Maya: From Cancún to City of Culture. World Heritage in Post-colonial Mesoamerica,' in D. Harrison and M. Hitchcock (eds.) *The Politics of World Heritage – Negotiating Tourism and Conservation*, Clevedon, Channel View Publications, 2005, pp. 35-49.

A new American dream: Taking the Celtic cure in mediated landscape

Monica Emerich

Introduction

In Boulder, Colorado, USA, there is a small, independent bookstore that has held its ground on the most coveted real estate in the city, remaining against all odds where other independent stores have folded. The store is what some would call New Age – it's a spiritual odyssey through the world's cultures and a feast for the senses as delicate tunes from a Celtic harp and heady scents from sacred Native American sage bundles envelop the bricoleur, the consumer, the cultural voyeur and the idle curiosity seeker. In the past fourteen years, during which I have fallen at least once into all of these categories of patronage at the store, the Celts have crept toward territorial victory on aisle two, flexing media muscle at neighboring UFO and extraterrestrial studies. Nestled against the peaks that punctuate the ending of the great plains of America and the beginning of the Rocky Mountains, Boulder is the venue for many a Celtic event, from Scottish shamans who heal depression to Irish priestesses bearing sacred waters from Brigid's holy well. The stores offer a dazzling array of Celtic goods – amulets, knots, athames, crosses, dragons, folk songs, power crystals, and bath salts – mostly marketed with a decidedly otherworldly, spiritual framing. Geo-spiritual constructions of 'Celticity' in American popular culture have spawned an explosion of self-curative media, from Mind/Body/Spirit books to divination tools to spiritual tourism websites. Anchoring these Celtic tales are the seminal fixtures of landscapes – standing stones, dolmens, caves and holy wells. Beltane, Lughnasa, Samhain, Imbolc and Yule have become ritual celebrations in a town where crusty cattle ranchers settled next door to ore miners and where the house from the Mork and Mindy television comedy is a stone's throw from the Buddhist temple.

Mostly these products, holidays, and visiting experts highlight the 'Celtic' part of their origins rather than the particulars of their lineage of Cornish, Scottish, Welsh, Manx, Irish or Breton. This falls into line with the ways in which traditional understandings of 'Celtic' – as a bounded reference to ethnicity, nationalism, geography, or culture – have been problematised and contextualised within polysemic discourses of individuals and groups. In the American New Age and Healthy Living media and marketplace, the term's cache seems to lie in its promise for a cure for the aches and pains of modernity. My research has focused on New Age and Healthy Living (alternative medicine, Mind/Body/Spirit goods and services, ecological/sustainable goods, and natural and organic products) media and markets and the intersection of media, religion and culture. That work revealed pervasive references to Celtic cultures and traditions (real or imagined). Mostly, these were contextualised as avenues to recover a lost way of life, wisdom or spirituality and very often any reference to Celticity was coupled with, even framed within, certain types of landscapes. As I collected more materials, I wondered how the constructions that were taking place might link with, impact or contradict the progenitors; those real objects in real spaces. This chapter therefore takes an auto-ethnographic approach to the study of spiritualised geographies in Cornwall. It is based on my personal experiences in 2002 when I obtained a six-week research fellowship to travel to Cornwall. My goal was to examine expressions of Celticity through the lens of cultural geography, media and religion.

Building a Spiritual Celticity through Landscape

People have always used the natural world as a way to orient themselves to 'ordinary and extraordinary powers, meanings and values', says Albanese.[1] These sorts of 'nature' narratives can reveal historical tensions in our relationships with political, social and economic structures that are built, literally and figuratively, on and through the natural world. From this broader notion of nature, we carve our landscapes – spaces that become places through the additional meanings we read into the site. In this sense, landscapes are 'texts' – semiotic systems that enable us to map ourselves with relation to the social world and the construction of private identity. As powerful reflectors of human desires and needs, landscapes are, like all material cultures, linked to man's inveterate quest for meaning and idealization and both need to be considered as mutually constructive.[2] Geographer J.B. Jackson in 1980 wrote that landscapes can serve as 'ethnic gardens' where we impart our own wisdom to the next generation.[3] They can serve as background for formal subjects inspired by myth or philosophy, as descriptive geography that seeks to make the world visible and inspire wonder, as theatre to amuse us, and as lenses through which we can gaze at histories and populations as well as reflexively order our own identities to time and space.

The interpretation of landscapes constructs many types of pilgrims, if we use that word in the sense of seekers who imbue landscapes with their intentionality whether directly through footfall on the path to Madron Well in West Penwith or indirectly through their participation in the marketplace of Celtic goods that informs and reproduces the broader economy, trade and image of Celticity. For my purposes, I was interested in how Celtic lands become a negotiated site of tradition located between received cultural memory and cultural memory-in-the-making through two populations who would claim some stakeholder status.

One approach to the analysis was through the idea of the Self. The notion of the person as a sort of built environment, as an individual with the power and the responsibility to shape him or herself, has evolved through the Enlightenment project and Cartesian dualism of mind vs. matter onward through the pressures, forms and events of late modernity. As part of this, the traditional systems by which people come to know themselves and their place in the world have shifted and been reshaped by the effects of globalization, capitalism, media, and rationality and the subsequent flows of symbols, people, labour, and capital across borders. The disembedding of local social systems and re-embedment in global ones have brought about the reflexive ordering and reordering of social relations whereby new networks across new spaces reshape old conceptions of affinities and identities into new interconnected webs of multiculturalism, transnationalism and plurality, Giddens says.[4] These dynamics are not experienced in the same way across populations but each has the potential to profoundly affect culture and systems of signification.

Media insert here, in the signifying process, as channels of transmission, banks of symbols, sites of symbolic exchange and production, and active generative and reflective agents of culture and identity. To elaborate on this latter point, media have been characterised, on the one hand, as determinative influences on passive audiences or, on the other hand, as benign mirrors of the real action going on 'out there' in the culture. Today, media are perceived as both, as active agents of culture, engaged dialectically with active receivers or users (audiences) in the construction, transformation, or modification of culture.[5] This is important when we consider how we build our identities. The globalised media provide a cultural bazaar of symbolic resources to individuals who (with varying degrees of agency dependent upon the variables of their social and physical geographies) peruse the histories and artifacts of cultures, including religious or spiritual traditions and landscapes. The circulation of these symbols and the nature of the media in general enable the decontextualization of landscapes and their reinsertion into our individualised identity narratives to be assembled and resorted in endless ways within the medium of the technology and the imagination of the individual user. The circulation of ideas about landscapes also plays a key role in the transformation of space into place.[6] Be it a hand-painted log of the hunt on the cavern wall or the blog of one woman's spiritual odyssey, these stories add to the public or consensus knowledge about a place and its conceptualization can then be re-enacted through imagery upon the website, one's backyard, and tour.[7] The ideas of things can become sacred through the circulation of 'myths', a term used by Barthes in 1972 to denote not falsehood but a science of forms (semiology) and an ideological construction (historical perspective).[8] These myths are sources of deep cultural meanings and they are circulated through media where their symbols and discourses become tools for the 'elaboration of the self'.[9] Through this myth-building, mediated process, places may become defined less by the uniqueness of their locations, landscape, and communities than by the focusing of experiences and intentions onto a particular setting. Celtic landscapes become bridges to optional ways of being and represent a discursive space within which to frame a lifestyle, values and identities.[10]

The Nature of Therapeutic Celticity

Bowman in 2000 wrote that while Celts were once the marginalised, living on the

periphery, they are now 'regarded as Noble Savages, less tainted by the ills of modern life, repositories of a spirituality, a sense of tradition, a oneness with nature that has elsewhere been lost'.[11] From the best-selling book *The Mists of Avalon* to the hundreds of adventure-spiritual tours devoted to rooting out the Celtic deities across Europe, American popular culture simmers with a Celtic, spiritual fever. Arthurian legends have been the stuff of childhood imagination for several generations and even our automobiles bear names such as Excalibur and Avalon; there might not be a product in this culture that understands the power of identity politics more than the auto industry. We expect our wheels to roll out our most prized images of American pluckiness, fortitude, bravery and positive psychology and we find Celtic legend perfectly suited to those semiotic needs. But these names also interestingly and overwhelmingly link to a different type of American dreaming.

The images of menhirs, fougos, stone circles, dolmen, Celtic crosses, quoits and holy wells and the sounds of Celtic music evoke a time and space outside of the market culture. For the 'Cardiac Celt' as Bowman describes those of us who 'just feel Celtic in our hearts', Celtic landscapes are often non-industrialised and non-commodified space.[12] These readings may mediate between disgruntlement with the so-called American Dream and its reformation of egalitarianism, community, and labour. These "texts" are both of the world and not-of-the-world. A website for a California-based tour operator says:

> Beautiful Cornwall is in the extreme southwestern part of Britain. Cornwall is a peninsula encircled by coastline that abounds with rugged cliffs, hidden bays, fishing villages, sandy beaches & sheltered coves where pirates & smuggling

A place of reflection (Photograph by Anna Tonkin)

> were once common. The Cornish people have a Celtic-Iberian origin, which still lives on in superstition, folklore & fairy tales. Come journey with us to mystical Cornwall – land of the Celts, Arthur, Goddesses, standing stones, earth mysteries, leylines, and mystery! A trip of a lifetime!![13]

There seems here more of a promise than just a physical respite from one's wage labour. There is the aura of magic-based thrill-seeking that pervades the popular culture and expresses an underlying melancholy for a more holistic life that draws equally on the mind, body and spirit, that regenerates society, that reclaims a place for mystery, and that reconfigures the boundaries between humans and the natural world.

American author Frank MacEowen's books are entitled *The Mist-Filled Path: Celtic Wisdom for Exiles, Wanderers, & Seekers*; *The Spiral of Memory & Belonging: A Celtic Path of Soul and Kinship*; and *The Celtic Way of Seeing: Meditations on the Irish Spirit Wheel*. Is it a yearning for 'a way to restore spontaneity, creativity and mystery, if these things are assumed to be necessary to humankind's fulfillment'?[14] In Boulder, I attended a sold-out event to hear a Scottish shaman speak about Celtic spirituality and the treatment of depression. The shaman explained that in the Celtic tradition and in the Gaelic language there is no identification of the self with the effect, as in 'I am depressed' which would be expressed instead as the 'depression is on me'. This different way of thinking, she explained, is also manifest in the manner in which the Celtic tradition of her lineage does not separate God from the self. 'When we lose the sacred,' she said, 'we fall into despair.' Rediscovering a way to incorporate the sacred into our lives, outside of institutionalised religion, is presented as an antidote to the subsumation by science, technology, and the market of our life world in the Healthy Living and New Age media. Be it Celtic or other indigenous or folk traditions, they present a counterposition to late modernity and a way to bridge the spheres of labour and leisure, subsistence and happiness, and sacred and profane.

The hyper-Celticised landscapes in these media are what Park in 1994 called 'enigmatic landscapes', places that hold antiquities and are subsequently heaped with layers of interpretations.[15] Through the media, we can envision background scenes around such landscapes to bring forth the sort of culture we want them to symbolise and in the media I examine, there is a heavy investment in backgrounds that are not our everyday. So, a long stone is more likely to be depicted in silhouette against a grassy knoll than in the midst of cow pasture holding up farm implements. Writing about 'the landscape of culture', Hall asks 'can we see Englishness without seeing, somewhere in our mind's eye, England's green and pleasant land, rose-trellised thatched cottages, village green and church steeple, a "sceptered isle"?'[16] These tropes are rooted in historical power-knowledge relationships, in struggles among classes and who gets to write official recorded history.

Landscapes are in 'a constant motion of social relations and power struggles' because they are embedded in the lived experience of local and distant populations involved with them.[17] We all read landscapes selectively, and this becomes ideological work that holds material power when those desires are expressed in practices. The selective reading of landscapes can exacerbate the museumification of cultures from one perspective

and become a liminal, transformative space, from another. The various readings of a landscape will impact local and distant populations differently depending upon other social realities, including the power of one nation's currency against another, political freedoms regarding travel and speech, and cultural mores, for example. The mediated representations of Celtic landscapes as portals to other dimensions that might be so liberating for American Celtic enthusiasts can also lead to the environmental degradation of distant lands via an onslaught of spiritual tourism. Alternatively, local populations might experience new views to the world, new economies, and new symbolic resources that enable their own, desired transformations. Intentionality does not necessarily manifest into reality and imaginings can quickly become destabilised when we attempt to put them into practice. In the case of my own visit to Tintagel in Cornwall, I had never visualised it as anything but preserved perfectly against its backdrop of crashing waves, never imagining and never forced to think about the living culture around it.

A Yank in Cornish 'Gardens'

As I pulled into the village of Tintagel, the first shockwaves registered: who had turned Merlin into a capitalist? His be-robed, be-spectacled, bearded self was everywhere I looked: on cups, on signs, on books and, in one case, embodied in the shop owner. The more I saw of him, the more I felt robbed of that intensely private moment when I would impose upon Tintagel the full force of my own dreaming, achieving a therapeutic moment when I would feel myself and the world to be different. Try as I might, however, I couldn't get the Merlinised shop owner out of my head. As I peered down at the castle, I felt conspicuous in my American accent and tourist gaze. What had I expected – to be the lone walker on the footpath? To be the only person on the face of the earth to know about the legend? A childhood of dreaming suddenly seemed quite silly.

St Cyor's Holy Well at Luxulyan (Photograph by Anna Tonkin

China clay works at Bugle in mid-Cornwall (Photograph by Anna Tonkin)

I was relaying this adventure to a dinner companion later that evening. A former Cornish china clay miner, he sighed and said, 'We aren't just a land of pixies and saints, you know' and he decided at that moment that I was in need of an education. The next morning we took a drive to a land that he found deeply meaningful as a spiritual compass point not only for himself but also as a Cornishman with a social history to be negotiated. The 'tips', those ridged white pyramids of the remains of china-clay mines, had I stumbled upon them alone, would have done little to move me. I hail from a land scarred with the pits and strips of mines. But standing at their edge with my guide, I was deeply moved at his respect for the mines and his sorrow at the loss of the china-clay industry. Many of these White Alps had been leveled, considered as blights on the landscape. He was truly puzzled as to why Cornwall's proud industrial heritage should be considered less Celtic than the region's holy wells, standing stones and Arthurian connections. Cornwall's industrial past holds a deep spiritual meaning as the source of nurture and identity, as I was reminded by the Christmas card I received years later from a Cornish friend that showed the ghostly silhouette of an abandoned Cornish tin mine.

My next tour guide in Cornwall was an official in the Anglican Church. Zipping his car through the winding roads, my guide explained that he found no antagonism between so-called Paganism and Christian traditions and freely embraced both in his parish church through festivals, field trips and liturgy. He took me to the graveyard of St Levan's church where a large, cleft boulder was flanked by a phallic-shaped tall stone. Amid the Christian crosses and headstones, these geologic wonders represented an alternate worldview to the Christian end-of-time scenario. One legend had it that when the cleft enlarged wide enough to allow a cart and horse to pass through, the end times were nigh, but the more ancient story embedded in the rocks was clear as the 'male' menhir rose sharply before the labial stone. We visited another small parish church at St Buryan. Inside the church, in each pew, were individualised prayer pillows cross-stitched by members of the congregation. One in particular caught my eye: it showed a shining, towering cross of gold bursting forth from the center of a standing stone circle. My own Celtic bias provided the first reading of the pillow as the blending of Pagan and Christian symbolism, but without interviewing its owner, it was impossible to know whether both the cross and the circle were considered spiritual or if the integration of the two simply reflected one or the other as a religious object embedded within a particular cultural and historical framework.

The search for spiritual Celtic landscapes resulted in delightfully open-ended interpretative performances. There were navigations to Carn Euny in a thick mist; to Madron Well past tattered clouties; to St Levan's hermitage ruin where I longed instead to run down the slope to join the bathers at sea; to Helman Tor where I saw in the rocks the shape of the rabbit goddess as I stood for photos with my Methodist hosts; to the Dragons and Saints Festival at a church, its name lost during a dizzying one-day tour of stone churches; to the solitary day spent at the Witchcraft museum in Boscastle; to Pendennis castle where I was treated to my first pasty; and to Gwennap Pit where I started to understand the full importance of Methodism in the county. As a result of those experiences, my own sense of Celtic has shifted.

I've asked other Americans who regularly seek out sacred Celtic places, experiences and objects why Celtic songs are described as hauntingly beautiful, Celtic trees as wise, and Celtic sea salts as healthier? Why are mists elsewhere portals to mysterious ecstasy when at home they are considered a damnable fog? Why are our Cottonwood trees 'big weeds'? It seems to hinge on the degree of familiarity – actually, unfamiliarity. The less we know about a society, a culture or a group, the more useful they are as vehicles for transportation out of our own everyday concerns, which are reflected back at us in our own green lawns (need mowing), our own gnarled trees (need pruning), our own fogged up windshields (need wiping), and our own table salt (needs dinner). The imagination of Celtic lands provides a relief from our ordinary and our imagining of them holds a sense of magic and 'the force of magic lies in its use of desire as a major contributing factor in causing hoped-for results'.[18] These geo-spiritual texts serve as conceptual stakes in the ground to declare that purposeful activity is occurring in our imagination.[19] But how to keep those stakes in the conceptual ground is another problem.

I overheard an American tourist who was visiting Cornwall complain about her earlier trip to Glastonbury, calling it a sad disappointment. The place, she said, was worse than Disneyland and she accused the village of becoming a caricature of itself, with shopkeepers relentlessly commodifying the sacred. She felt cheated and disoriented. I could imagine the type of experience she had in mind as she climbed the Tor or visited the Chalice Well, hoping that some small magic would make itself known. If the spiritual experience is articulated in terms of the anticipated results, as Grimes says, one of those surely is the hope for a launch-pad from which to begin a private journey of self

Madron Well in West Cornwall (Photograph by Sarah Chapman)

improvement and change. And even if commodified culture is the avenue through which we first approach, inform and shape our Celtic spiritual ideal, we bracket out that market culture in hopes it won't contaminate our experience. Media may provide a private space for imagination, but reinserting those internal reflections into a public space is often less accommodating, and real-world contact with spaces and places means possible ruptures in the hull of our dreams, and that can be both a lucky and unlucky happenstance.

Conclusion

A friend and I celebrated a final evening in the Duchy, calling a taxi to ferry us back to our lodgings late in the evening. Our driver was an amiable fellow and we struck up a conversation. He was a fisherman like his father and his grandfather and great-grandfather before that. He still fished but the seas were not as productive and the work didn't pay so well any longer. He asked us what we thought of Cornwall and we glanced furtively at each other in the backseat. How to explain the juxtaposition of the Cornwall that had been produced in our American imaginations through du Maurier, Victoria Holt, Celtic New Age, and Arthurian legend and the Cornwall that we had been fortunate enough to find?

We told him that we arrived with our own mythologies and that while some of those remained intact, most were changed, tempered by the walk through others' sacred gardens. We had developed a new appreciation of and patience for the tourists to our own homeland who come searching for the Wild West of cowboys and Indians. We laughed at some of our experiences, like fox hunts, for example. We'd been traveling to Lanyon Quoit when our driver encountered an assemblage of hunters on the road and waited patiently for them to make a move, which took a good bit of time. We were stunned. It was so British, after all, and being vegetarians we despise animal cruelty. 'You are so American,' growled our guide who couldn't take our protestations any longer. The fox is a pest. The foxhunt is a long cultural tradition and as much a part of country life as were the stone circles for which we were using up good petrol to visit, we were told.

We explained to our taxi driver about our bungled attempts to find Dozmary Pool and ending up in someone's garden, of our passing over the beauty of Bodmin Moor in a myopic hunt for Jamaica Inn, of the apologies we would deliver to our relatives who each year want to visit Buffalo Bill's grave as we grumble about the slaughter of bison and colonization of Native American land. He smiled at all of this and suddenly turned the wheel and plunged onto a small bumpy road leading into a pasture. We were slightly alarmed but the car lights revealed some small stones. These were the stuff of dreams of his childhood, the Ring and the Thimble, and the stones across his lands were as much a part of his identity, his memory of himself and his place in the world, as were the seas. Our stories co-mingled, each providing new context for the next, building on each other's experiences and memories. It was, like any good conclusion, a moment of synthesis. In that space, our various Celticities stood as the collage, the reflection of 'sympathies, antipathies, and chains of influence', as Sack has said, in accordance to our human needs, desires and praxis, the social structures and determinations that defined our particular roles in the moment.[20] We all had found a therapeutic imaginary in a land to dream on.

Notes

1. C. Albanese, *Nature Religion in America*, University of Chicago Press, 1990, p. 8.
2. R. Bendix, *Max Weber: An Intellectual Portrait*, Methuen & Co. Ltd, 1959, p. 481.
3. J.B. Jackson, *The Necessity for Ruins*, University of Massachusetts Press, 1980, pp. 34-35.
4. A. Giddens, *The Consequences of Modernity*, University of Stanford Press, 1990, pp. 16-17.
5. J. Carey, *Communication as culture: Essays on media and society*, Unwin-Hyman, 1988.
6. E. Relph, *Place and Placelessness*, Pion Limited, 1976.
7. *Ibid.*
8. R. Barthes, *Mythologies*, Hill and Wang, 1972.
9. W.C. Roof, *Spiritual marketplace*, Princeton University Press, 1999.
10. J.P. Bartkowski and W.S. Swearingen, 'God meets Gaia in Austin, Texas: A case study of environmentalism as implicit religion', *Review of Religious Research*, 38, 4, p. 313.
11. M. Bowman, 'Contemporary Celtic Spirituality' in A. Hale and P. Payton (eds.), *New Directions in Celtic Studies*, University of Exeter Press, 2000, p. 74.
12. *Ibid*, p. 70. See also M. Bowman, 'Cardiac Celts' in G. Harvey and C. Hardman (eds.), *Paganism Today*, Thorsens, 1995.
13. http://nccn.net/~wwithin/walesengcorn. html
14. P. Brantlinger, *Bread and circuses: Theories of mass culture as social decay*, Cornell University Press, 1983, p. 146.
15. C. Park, *Sacred Worlds: An Introduction to Geography and Religion*, Routledge, 1994.
16. S. Hall, 'New Cultures for Old' in D. Massey and P. Jess (eds.), *A Place in the World*, pp. 176-211, Oxford University Press, 1995, p. 183.
17. D. Mitchell, *The Lie of the Land*, University of Minnesota Press, 1996, p. 28.
18. R.L. Grimes, *Ritual Criticism: Case Studies in Its Practice, Essays on Its Theory*, University of South Carolina Press, 1990, p. 49.
19. R.L. Grimes, 'Ritual' in W. Braun and R. T. McCutcheon (eds.), *Guide to the Study of Religion*, Cassell, 2000, p. 266.
20. Sack quoted in Park, *Sacred Worlds*, 1994, p. 8.

Tourism and the Cornish Alps

Jesse Harasta

Some landscapes and places demand attention: they are too big, too shocking, too different to be ignored and the Cornish Clay Country is just such a place. The pits and tips demand interpretation. A growing body of work is emerging that studies the literature and cultural traditions of the Clay Country, but this essay aims to approach it from a different direction.[1] Instead of examining the Clay Country 'Culture,' it instead takes as its point of examination the public interpretation of that landscape. I examine the two primary locations where interpretations of the landscape and its meaning for today's society are presented to the public: the Eden Project and the Wheal Martyn China Clay Museum. These museums articulate well-developed, contrasting opinions about the Clay Country and are the two largest venues in the region. I will show how these two sites embody two discourses, which I call the Eco-Restorationist and the Industrial Triumphalist, and how these discourses take on unique dynamics within Cornwall due to the distinctive ethnic makeup and ambiguous place of Cornwall and the Cornish in Britain.

Cornwall and Clay

The Clay Country landscape of mountainous tips and canyon-like pits has long been a matter of considerable pride for many in the area. The logo of English China Clays, the primary producer until 1999, was of two side-by-side pyramids, one pointing up and dark (the tip) and the other pointing downwards and light (the pit). The ability to master the natural landscape at times led to a perspective verging on haughtiness. In 1978 Daphne du Maurier, the famous author and resident of Cornwall, wrote the introduction to a history of the industry in which she said:

> Environmentalists beware! A visitor remarked to me, a while past, staring across at the ships berthed in Par Harbour and the growing expanse of dockland, then beyond to the China Clay country itself, with pyramid and cone outlined against the skyline, 'don't you think all this is a blight on the countryside?' A

> blight! I nearly choked in answer. [...] As for those hills themselves, stark, austere, an enduring proof of what men had wrestled from them through the years, let my environmental visitor try to flatten them, sow grass-seed, and turn them from living monuments to the audacity and courage of generations of working men into a 'pleasure-ground' or park.[2]

Despite her challenge environmentalists have articulated powerful criticisms of the China Clay Country and have had great success in forcing the industry itself to convert tips and pits into 'pleasure-grounds'. As early as 1975, the *Western Morning News* reported that English China Clays was converting a 'sterile concentration of pits, tips and other odd industrial sorts' into green heathland suitable for agriculture.[3] Since then, former industrial areas have been converted into football pitches, wildlife habitats, walking trails and heathland.[4]

The greatest 'pleasure-ground', probably far beyond what Daphne du Maurier imagined, is the Eden Project. Built in the bottom of Bodelva Pit on the outskirts of the Clay Country, the Eden Project bills itself as a 'Living Theatre of Plants'. The brainchild of Tim Smit, an ex-recording industry executive, Eden has inherited much of its founder's flair for self-promotion: everything is grand, big, bold, unprecedented, and experimental. The gardens and grounds constitute one of the largest tourist attractions in Cornwall, drawing in hundreds of thousands each year.[5] But the Eden Project aims at being much more than a plant theme park. Via displays through the Biomes and the outreach of the Eden Foundation, the organization aims to turn itself into a metaphor for the complete transformation of society. The central image of this metaphor is the conversion of the Bodelva China Clay pit into Eden. I will show that in doing so, Eden articulates with an Eco-Restorationism discourse which has a particular manifestation in Cornwall and implication for Cornish communities, especially those still linked to extractive industries, such as in the Clay Country around Eden.

The Eden Project

The metaphor of Eden begins before one arrives at the gates. For example, the large Ayr Holiday Park in St Ives provides this description of the Eden Project on its website: 'The Eden Project has become the symbol of all that is modern and innovative in Cornwall. It also leads the way in education about sustainability, culture and climate change across the world'.[6]

Those who miss the metaphor before their arrival quickly encounter it as they enter Eden. One of the first signs all visitors sees is an aerial photo of the former china clay pit with the line 'If you believe…' and a second image showing the same shot with a completed Eden and the line 'there should be a place'. It continues with: 'that explores what a great future might look like/that celebrates life/and puts champagne in the veins'. The gray, grim picture of the pit contrasts with the liveliness and brilliant colours of the other photos. This is repeated over the ticket booths where there is a huge picture of the pit labelled '1998'. Again the message is repeated at an overlook where one enjoys one's first view of the domes themselves; visitors have been conveniently provided with an interpretative sign with only a picture of the old pit with 'December 1998' writ-

ten on it. Similarly, in the membership recruitment room there is a poster that reads: 'What we are' with a large image of the pit from 1995 and the caption 'Many things are possible. You can make things happen if you go for it. Here's Eden back in 1995'.

Similarly, at the theatre that plays the Eden video the show starts with contrasting fly-over shots of the old pit and grim music. This is followed by images of flowers and exotic guest performers in bright-coloured indigenous clothing. The video returns to 1997 and has grim voices and music over large machines, flowing clay and monitors. Tim Smit describes it as 'a very horrific example of our industrial culture at its worst …it ripped people and landscape apart. This is an example of turning that around'. Later it would show a time elapsed image of the pit transforming.

The repeated refrain is a simple one: begin with post-industrial devastation, add to it tremendous energy, creativity and hope and out of it emerges a new bloom. In this new world, plants grow, children laugh, people dance and everyone lets go of their restraint and dour moods. Eden is an embodiment of this metaphor – even the name evokes both original innocence and joy, 'Eden', and the intense labour, the 'Project', needed to achieve it once again. Moreover, if successful 'we' will return to that state ourselves: our lives will become more spontaneous, more filled with art, more colourful. The tightly manicured grounds and the ever-present abundance of staff members speak to the tremendous energy put into Eden, conveying the message that regeneration of the natural world can happen, but it won't be easy and it won't occur on its own.

In this scheme, Cornwall has an ambiguous place and is relegated to the under-used periphery of the site. Most of the displays in the 'Wild Cornwall' section detail the Eden Project's enormous efforts to restore the natural landscape of Cornwall from the wounds left by the mining industry. Even these displays are not only relegated to the edges, but are left under tended, to weather in the sun and rain. To emphasise

The Domes of Eden (Photograph by Anna Tonkin)

Cornwall as more natural, or even as different to England, would undermine both the metaphor of post-devastation rebirth and the idea of a shared 'industrial culture'. Cornwall must belong to 'us' and it must be ruined for the story of Eden to work.

Wheal Martyn

Across a landscape of pits and tips from Eden lies the only other large tourist attraction to focus on the interpretation of the Clay Country. The Wheal Martyn China Clay Country Museum is a reconstruction of a pre-1950s China Clay processing plant. Funded by the industry it aims to be a showcase of traditional mining techniques and the distinctive culture that has emerged out of them. The Museum is divided into several sections. The first is a new area with a café, shop, atrium for the display of art and a number of displays on culture. After this building, one enters the open-air section. From here there are two options, the 'Historic Trail' which leads through the historic buildings of the clayworks and the 'Nature Trail' over the recovering wastelands. Both trails link up higher up on the hill and lead to a third area, the 'Pit View' where one is able to see into the two modern clay pits.

In the Historic Trail, the primary emphasis is upon technology. There is little in the way of cultural context, instead it is a space to show off restored water wheels and clay drying areas. The displays discuss the techniques used to 'win' the clay, the products produced out of it and an elaborate transportation system. The Nature Trail is unique amongst the museum's displays, as it has almost no interpretative signs. Instead, it first passes through a children's play area and then winds up through ruins. A handful of bits of old clay workings have been cut out of the rhododendrons where they sit decaying. Despite the name 'nature trail', the only signage here describes the ruins, not the natural world.

Travelling from one to another, the Museum and Eden appear to be in some form of indirect dialogue with one another. The 'nature trail' is a fine example of this. Eden is based upon the premise that industry – clay mining being an example – has caused such incredible devastation upon the earth that only a heroic effort can rescue it. Wheal Martyn's response is clever, but subtle. By taking visitors through a lush grove of rhododendrons studded with ruins, it says that nature has come back of its own accord and that the clay industry is in the long-term harmless. This is only expressed outwardly at in the guidebook, which reads:

> The extraction of China Clay from the granite of mid Cornwall over the last two hundred years has dramatically changed the landscape of this area. [...] The Wheal Martyn site has also been affected by this. The Nature Trail passes through the grounds of two china clay works which have had their share of ecological problems brought about by human influence. However, wildlife soon returned to these areas once the clay works closed.[7]

The guide gives a list of numerous flowers, animals and birds one might see, but in my visit the only species I saw was rhododendron. Despite being the most dominant form of plant in the area by far, this invasive alien is not featured in any of the sketches and descriptions and while they describe the area as part of natural succession, they also

Statues outside Wheal Martyn China Clay Museum (Photograph by Anna Tonkin)

note at one point that 'the Rhododendron plants are beginning to dominate the other species in this area'.[8] Of course, to admit that the 'natural restoration' of the tips led to colonization by an invasive plant would undermine the simplicity of their argument much as a celebration of any type of Cornish culture would undermine Eden's implicit argument that industry shatters communities.

Eco-Restorationists, Industrial Triumphalists

The 'conversation' between Eden and Wheal Martyn appears because they each articulate a distinctive discourse regarding the China Clay Country and our relationship to it. They do not need to address one another because by addressing the landscape, they join into an existing argument. Eden builds upon an earlier discourse where Cornwall, and in particular the town of St Ives, is portrayed as a place for escape, rejuvenation and recreation. There is a long-standing image of the seaside Cornish holiday and its power to heal the psychic wounds of fast-paced, industrial society upon English men and women. It is a short step from this point to the premise of the Eden Project: the healing of the entire society from the wounds of industry. This perspective increasingly clashes with an indigenous Cornish identity, which is closely related to a history of industrial prowess.

This formulation where Cornwall is natural and the place to build a new life or develop a new society I call the Eco-Restorationist Discourse. More than a set of academic arguments, it is an approach to the land that becomes embodied in the stories and actions of individuals across Cornwall. To illustrate this point, I will relate examples from a formal interview and a few more from informal conversations I have had.[9] In the summer of 2009 I spoke to a woman who had spent much of her life in London. She had come to Cornwall on holiday before moving down and spoke of the joys of staying in St Ives. She told me how she desired to 'downsize' her life, leaving a good-paying job in the information sector and moving into a small cottage far from any towns. She became involved in environmental activism and related to me the problems she faced trying to drag the locals into the project: she said they were too compliant to the local powers-that-be to get involved. She said that environmental activism can be tied to the preservation of ancient monuments because they give a positive message, but the fascination with mining history for her had connotations of classism and industrial exploitation.

In addition to in-depth interviews, I have had a number of shorter conversations on trains and buses throughout Cornwall on these issues. So often, the refrain of visitors from England was of the joys of St Ives. I met a young couple on break from university in Bristol who came down every year to visit St Ives, Eden and the Tate Museum. She in particular loved St Ives, especially for its light, which she said was perfectly captured within the Tate building. I met an elderly couple from the Midlands who always stayed in St Ives. They never travelled out of Penwith in their trips and were experts on the St Ives hotels. In contrast, I met a Cornishwoman from Penzance who travelled to the Clay Country to have her hair done as there wasn't in her estimate a proper salon in western Cornwall; she told me she never went to St Ives as it was 'too commercial' and fake. This discourse of rejuvenation and escape from a reality crops up in many situations. For example, in Cornwall many houses are given names by their owners and homes like 'Dream Achieved' or 'Shangri-La' speak to Cornwall as an otherworldly refuge and escape.

Wheal Martyn, on the other hand, embodies a wider discourse I call 'Industrial Triumphalism'. This is the glorious celebration of the wonders of industry, which we saw in the quote by du Maurier. The commemoration of industrial Cornwall is seen in Museum's fascination with technology and the tip-and-pit icon of English China Clays. However, it reaches far beyond the Museum. For instance, industry is celebrated in the Trevithick Day Festival, where antique steam engines are used to celebrate the invention of the locomotive. Likewise, the former Cornwall County Council supported the creation of the Cornish Mining World Heritage Site. The Council has invested considerable funding in having the mining districts recognised by the UN and supports preservation and cultural activities aimed at promoting the celebration and awareness of the mining past.

Discourse and Ethnicity

In Cornwall, this industrial narrative takes on an ethnic flavour as Cornishness is often associated with work within the earth. I will give two examples of this from interviews to show the depth that ethnicity and labour are intertwined in the minds of some

Cornish folk. In an interview with an elderly mine engineer, I inquired as to why the mines hold such power for people in Cornwall, despite their decline. He replied:

> It's in our blood. My father was a miner. His father was a miner. And his father [...] and so it goes back. And the fact that you probably see in some, a lot of the photographs in the library or somewhere, I don't know, the way they worked in those days, just little narrow tunnels, hundreds and hundreds of feet below ground. But there was perhaps two or three miners together, so that they three was a little family if you like.

Neither Eden nor Wheal Martyn made explicitly ethnic arguments about the landscape. However, in the climate of Cornwall, where mining heritage is so often grounded in ethnicity, any interpretation of the Clay County becomes ethnically charged. Eden is a physical representation of a discourse that is self-consciously eco-friendly, but unconsciously English and middle class. In it, Cornwall (and the Westcountry generally) is the site for the healing and re-creation of the English nation and the absolution of the English of their crimes against the land. In this discourse, the active agents are mobile, energetic and well-to-do English folk. Like all forms of capitalism, this restorationist, eco-capitalism celebrates the Herculean triumphs of the individual entrepreneur. It should come to no surprise that with the symbol of Eden comes the figure of Tim Smit. Through their work, they drag the stumbling, hesitant populace into the green knowledge-based economy of the future.

Yet, the 'populace' here includes many who see themselves as Cornish, not English. In the process of denouncing of what they see as broken, servile, surly, uneducated and poor within their own society, the Eco-Restorationists exacerbate conflict and misunderstanding between the ethnic groups and social classes of Cornwall. For the clay pit that they proudly eliminated to create Eden was not universally considered 'a very horrific example of our industrial culture at its worst'. For those who thought of the tips and pits as 'living monuments to the audacity and courage' of workers, the discourse of Eden erases the meaning of their communities' labour and denies the reality they feel 'in their blood.'

Notes

1. Philip Payton and Shelley Trower (eds.), *Cornish Studies: Seventeen*, University of Exeter Press, 2009. See also Clay Edition of *Cornish Story*, Autumn 2011.
2. Daphne du Maurier, 'Foreword' in Philip Varcoe, *China Clay: The Early Years*, 1978, p. 5.
3. James Mildren, 'How White were our Hillsides?', *Western Morning News*, 1975.
4. Charles Thurlow, *China Clay from Cornwall and Devon: The Modern China Clay Industry*, 4th edition, St Austell: Cornish Hillside Publications, 2005, pp. 58-62. See also John R. Smith, *Cornwall's China Clay Heritage*, Twelveheads Press, 1992.
5. Martin Jackson, Eden: *The First Book, Eden Project*, 2000. See also Martin Jackson, *Eden: The Second Book Watch Us Grow*, Eden Project Books, 2002.
6. Ayr Holiday Park. Electronic document, http://www.ayrholidaypark.co.uk/st-ives/attractions-in-cornwall.php (accessed 20 June 2009).
7. Wheal Martyn China Clay Museum Guidebook, p. 24.
8. *Ibid*, p. 31.
9. The research for the remainder of this article is based upon 35 interviews which were conducted by the author in Cornwall between 2006 and 2011.

Genius Loci: Landscape, Legend and Locality; the role of folklore in the farming and fishing communities of the Rame peninsula, 1850–1950

Robert Keys

'... within this notion of people and place, story is the correspondence between the two. It informs our lives. It keeps things known. It is the umbilical cord between the past, the present and the future'.[1]

When does land become landscape? Why do people claim to experience a 'spirit of place'? How does a 'real' event become a local legend and perhaps eventually a folk tale? On the Rame peninsula the land has been shaped by an underlying geology and the enduring pressure of climate and weather, it has also been inescapably moulded by the life and labour of the communities that lived and worked upon it. Landscape implies a perception of land and an imagined relation to locality.[2] This imagined relation to landscape adds to a sense of place by way of the narratives associated with a locality and provides the spatial context for the folklore of a community. Recent work on folklore has indicated a renewed interest not just in the collection of oral evidence and the structural analysis of tales, but in the social history and ethnography of folklore. The on-going significance of re-telling popular folk tales, as well as the emergence and transmission of new urban legends, provides a valuable insight into community narratives.[3] This chapter will summarise a number of folk tales and legends associated with an area of south-east Cornwall and examine the way 'story' establishes a correspondence between a community and its history through a sense of place.[4]

Cornwall as a whole has often been seen as imbued with a unique 'Celtic spirit of place'; a spiritual legacy that tourism was not slow to exploit, even as far back as the advertising of Great Western Railways at the start of the twentieth century.[5] The folklore legacy of the fishing and farming communities scattered around the villages of Portwrinkle, Crafthole and Sheviock is the object of this investigation. The focus is

Portwrinkle by William Daniell, c 1820. From A Voyage Round Great Britain, in 8 volumes(1821-1825 edition)

whether folklore can be said to impart a particular 'spirit of place' to the area. The natural boundaries of the locality are the rivers Tamar and Lynher and the villages of Tideford and St Germans to the north, while the western extent of the area being considered is the Seaton river valley (in Cornish Nant Seythin) that runs from Hessenford to Downderry. This area (indicated in the map) is often referred to as 'Cornwall's Forgotten Corner'.[6] The chapter is based on evidence collected in the form of oral tradition, family photographs and legends. These were encountered while researching the Poor Man's Endeavour; a fishermans' cooperative that worked at Portwrinkle from the mid-nineteenth to the early twentieth centuries.[7] The original fishermens' cottages and the terraces for the coastguards have been largely preserved including the cottage of a real smuggling organiser, Thomas Helman. However, what had been a small settlement expanded dramatically in the last quarter of the twentieth century. The original working community has all but disappeared.

The chapter is also based on the author's childhood memories of folktales, family legends and anecdotes based on 'real' events in the villages from the 1950s and 1960s that were in the process of being 'folklorised', some of which have passed into the collective memory of the older members of the local community. The aim is not therefore to identify simply 'old' and therefore 'genuine' oral folk traditions that have somehow survived.[8] Although these are a significant feature of the area and much less well-known than the 'hearthside tales' of west Cornwall made famous by the nineteenth century collections of Hunt and Bottrell.[9] Instead the intention is to examine the on-going role of folklore in the cultural life of a community. A distinctive aspect will be the context in which such narratives could be creatively adapted to new events and why particular landscape features and local characters are used to embed the anecdotes and

tales in the collective memory. The folkloric creativity of kinship networks in circulating the 'best' legends and tales provides an important insight into notions of custom, popular rights and even 'justice in common' at the local level.[10] This 'subaltern' cultural tradition may be at odds with official narratives of the well-ordered local community and its more respected representatives; the village constable, the rector, the magistrate, the head-teacher or the doctor.[11] All served as figures of authority and a kind of paternalism but were also 'symbolic' representatives at the local level of more distant mechanisms of law and order. In contrast the protagonists of both traditional and more modern tales are often ambivalent figures, daring but not entirely admirable; the bawdy priest, the devious lawyer, the lawless aristocrat, the smuggler or the over venturesome young lad or maiden and the troubles they encounter. In general they would seem to be the breakers of local custom rather than its upholder and hence the moral lesson of the punishment they receive for their actions. Good tellers of tales could be almost anyone, but publicans, poachers, travelling salesmen and returning sailors were normally good for a story as were the village constable, the gamekeeper and local farmers with kinship roots in their community.[12] The economic centre of the fishing community at Portwrinkle was the fishermen's cooperative; the Poor Man's Endeavour, whose socio-economic history I have described elsewhere.[13]

The Rame peninsula for most of the medieval and early modern period was a landscape of farms, small village settlements and churchtowns, where the principal form of employment was agriculture, with some local quarrying, as in the blue elvan quarries on the river Lynher below Tideford. Along the coastal and river passages fishing settlements and some maritime trade and commerce flourished in the small harbours. Until the mid-nineteenth century the economic activity that shaped the landscape was char-

Thomas Helman's cottage in Portwrinkle (Photograph by Robert Keys)

acterised by the crafts and labour processes that underpinned and determined the working groups in agriculture and fishing. The next important feature was the kinship network that linked the labouring and small farmer families across the village and parish boundaries. Also important were the confessional affiliations that had divided most parishes between the established Anglican Church and the dissenting Methodist chapel since the eighteenth century. By the nineteenth century popular political loyalties, in so far as they are known, seem to have followed or been divided along the fracture lines of the local elites, particularly reflecting the influence and patronage of the landed interest. There were three significant estates; the Eliots of Port Eliot at St Germans, the Carews (later Pole Carews) of Antony and the Edgecombes of Cotehele and Mount Edgecombe. One of the Killigrews, who were sometime resident at Ince Castle, also deserves a mention here, for although the story is located on the far side of the river Lynher, local tradition links Henry Killigrew to a version of the Bluebeard legend. Alongside the stately homes of the aristocracy there were a number of imposing houses such as Wolsdon near Antony, which for many years had been held by the Deeble Bojer family, the location of another tale; while the Edgecombes feature in a legend once widely distributed in the locality. Aristocratic behavior or misbehaviour, as well as that of the clergy are an interesting recurrent theme in some of the legends.

The fishing rights were also controlled in part by the estates or the Duchy and both farmers and fishermen paid their tithe to the 'established' church of each parish, whether they considered themselves Anglicans or Dissenters; a recurrent bone of contention within the community. Nevertheless this was a rural and coastal landscape that the outside observer might well perceive as picturesque and tranquil.

The significant change that has transformed and obliterated the local fishing community occurred in the last half of the twentieth century and was due to two factors; tourism with its need for holiday lets and second homes and the growing demand for coastal retirement homes. Due to a failure to list the historic fish cellars they were allowed to fall into such a state of disrepair that it was relatively easy for a developer to move in and effectively destroy its historical integrity and any archaeological value that remained. They are now luxury apartments complete with hot tubs and coastal views and underground parking spaces for residents.

There is always a danger when describing a disappearing world to sentimentalise and misrepresent the complexity of a community, simply through the process of selecting the evidence. I am particularly aware of this in dealing with folk tales and folklore, gathered from family members and local acquaintances, which may create the impression of an isolated, pre-modern community dominated by irrational and superstitious beliefs. In fact many of the tales were and are recounted in the context of popular entertainment within the family, at the pub or in the workplace. Most families had members who had worked overseas or served overseas in the armed forces and thanks to the British Empire were familiar with far more exotic corners of the world than many average urban or industrial workers of the time. This is also reflected in another type of tale focusing on the adventures of family members fighting the Boers in South Africa, or the Boxers in China, experiencing the 'Wild West' in the mining centres of Montana and Colorado or, closer to home, the 'dockyard' tales of those who worked in the naval yard at Devonport. In short tales which often cut across the categories of earlier folklorists searching for archaic survivals, but were part of the social intercourse of a community, rather than a solemn rehearsal of past events.

Before examining some of the local folk tales in relation to place and landscape, it is important to consider how folklore is defined in academic work and acknowledge the very different theoretical approaches to this material. Modern folklorists operate with a clear distinction between legend; a narrative which claims to be based on fact and even on personal experience and folk tale; which whether traditional or a re-telling of traditional material is understood by the teller and the audience as a fictional performance. As Linda Degh pointed out this can be traced back to the distinction made by Von Sydow and his followers between 'memorates' and 'fabulates'.[14] The academic analysis of the material described here would require the systematic application of such theoretical distinctions if the aim was simply to classify. In everyday usage however, tales, anecdotes and stories are treated as synonymous and the systematic use of the terms memorate and fabulate; legend and folktale or fairy story, would confuse rather than clarify for the reader the continuing role of tales and legends in the community. The general approach to folklore here is that discussed by Gramsci in his *Prison Notebook* entries on folklore:

> Folklore should instead be studied as a conception of the world and life implicit in determinate strata of society (in time and space) and in ... opposition to official conceptions of the world ... that have succeeded one another in the historical process.[15]

For this reason the kind of linguistic analysis of a corpus of classic fairy stories in the tradition of Vladimir Propp will not be attempted.[16] The emphasis is more ethnographic and focuses on the social and cultural context rather than on the classification and analysis of individual texts. What cannot be ignored is the legacy of nineteenth century folklore collectors in Cornwall for the subsequent Celto-Cornish Revival.[17] This in turn permeated significant sections of literate working-class men and women in the aftermath of the Victorian and Edwardian advances in popular education. An interest in history, identity and community was no longer to be confined to an elite. How was spirit of place perceived in relation to the local landscape? How was it experienced both by settled communities in Cornwall, but also in the nostalgic memories of Cornish overseas migrants, anxious to maintain links with an imagined but increasingly distant homeland?

The 'genius loci' of the ancients had been conceived as real, albeit supernatural, beings. The gods were far away but the local spirits were all around us, at least until the scepticism of the Enlightenment and the scientific revolution reduced them to subjective hallucinations or an entirely fictional existence. These ambivalent spirits, like the Dondo in one local legend, had inhabited particular places in the woodlands, springs and mountains, unlike the more benevolent guardian spirits of hearth and home. The nature of their habitations, outside civilization and the community, indicates an important aspect of their being; from another world, beyond the pale of settlement and hence

Above: The fish cellars at Portwrinkle (Photograph by Robert Keys)
Below: Modern re-development of the cellars (Photograph by Robert Keys)

their function in any cultural narrative. The long transformation of the ancient pagan world by Christianity had expelled most of these 'spirits of place' to the netherworld or to the ambiguous realm of faeries and 'buccas', while the later Reformation of the sixteenth century tried to dispel them altogether. In the ancient world wildness and waste (vasta) was much more all pervasive and threatening to precarious subsistence-based communities than it is today. Even in the medieval world land was yet to become landscape, 'Nature' was yet to be cultivated and subdued. Only much later did the representation of land become the object of aesthetic contemplation as idealised 'landscape' and only later still in the work of sentimental and romantic poets and artists did such representations become particularised as 'The Lakes' or 'The Alps', or indeed the 'Cornish Riviera'. Thus painted and poetical scenes and vistas would draw in the cultivated observer and eventually the package tourist leading them to visit the originals. In this context for example one of the earliest images we have of Portwrinkle is a print from an early nineteenth century Daniell engraving, part of a series of coastal views of Britain available in expensive albums, but also in cheaper single prints designed with the mass market in mind.

Raymond Williams has observed that the village community and its landscape was viewed increasingly with nostalgia, a disappearing world, the repository of both traditional and natural organic values; a world of residual folklore and folk song.[18] In Britain the ancient naiads and dryads of the classical world had long been assimilated and transformed by the church and native tradition into the fairies, elves and sprites of medieval legend; Queen Mab, Puck and Robin Goodfellow.[19] In Cornwall the buccas and faeries of Celtic tradition lived on in the folk tales and fairy stories, which almost every parish could claim as its own. It is not surprising that in this long process of aesthetic transformation the 'genius loci' was reduced to the subjective experience of 'spirit of place' rather than the more threatening 'spirits from another place'. It was this 'spirit' that provided the sentimental bond of attachment to an imagined landscape and community, particularly for those forced by economic pressure to emigrate. The same sentimental bond that drives the descendants of the Cornish diaspora to return to their 'roots', if only for a short visit.

It is not the case that the Rame area was particularly isolated or backward. Historical research shows that folk beliefs and rituals had a declining significance for the fishing and farming communities of Britain in the late nineteenth and early twentieth centuries, if we mean by this sincerely held residual beliefs in faeries, ghosts and spectres, or faith in omens, charms and prophecies.[20] Political loyalties and ideologies as well as religious affiliations already had a more determining role, as did the growing interest of the educated common man in both science and indeed scientific socialism. Nevertheless legends and tales were remembered and recounted and provided entertainment in an age before the arrival of electricity, radio and television. Whether such tales were authentic and local, springing from oral tradition or had already come back into the culture adapted from a literacy source is not always possible to tell. Such sources would include the earlier published collections of folklorists and the short stories of local and regional writers published in works such as Doidges *Westcountry Almanac*, publications which were often forwarded to those overseas who wanted to

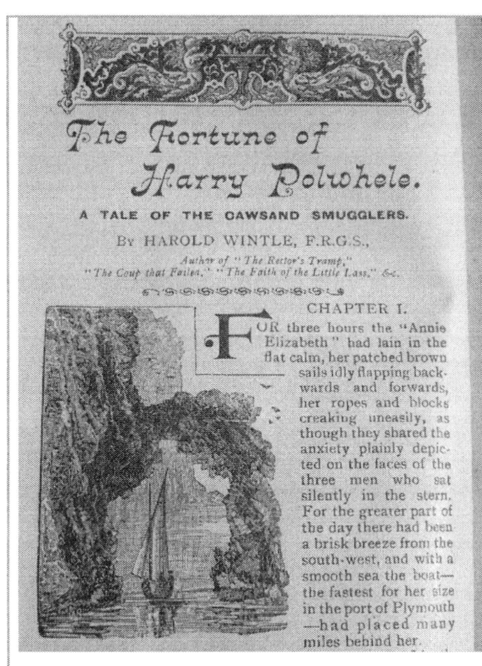

The Fortune of Harry Polwhele.

A TALE OF THE CAWSAND SMUGGLERS.

By HAROLD WINTLE, F.R.G.S.,

Author of "The Rector's Tramp," "The Coup that Failed," "The Faith of the Little Lass," &c.

CHAPTER I.

FOR three hours the "Annie Elizabeth" had lain in the flat calm, her patched brown sails idly flapping backwards and forwards, her ropes and blocks creaking uneasily, as though they shared the anxiety plainly depicted on the faces of the three men who sat silently in the stern. For the greater part of the day there had been a brisk breeze from the south-west, and with a smooth sea the boat—the fastest for her size in the port of Plymouth—had placed many miles behind her.

The Fortunes of Harry Polwhele *by Harold Wintle, an example of popular narrative*

keep abreast of local events.[21] These local almanacs, journals and occasional publications are an invaluable source at the local and regional level for the social historian investigating the links between local identities and the constitution of national identity, which often embedded distinctive regional elements in narratives of the nation and the 'national' popular culture.[22] Already romantic and sentimental narratives featuring smugglers, feisty heroines and local legends were in circulation.

Such literary narratives were complemented by the genuine folk creativity of amateur tellers of folktales, who shaped new oral narratives around local events and characters. These included the sighting of ghosts and unnatural happenings, as well as observations on local tragedies, crimes, acts of unusual bravery or even of unusual foolishness. In short the content of many of the narratives still to be found in popular culture and in the genres by which these are represented in the press and on television today; adventure, crime and detection, true romance and even horror stories and the supernatural. The tales described below all relate to or cluster around particular features of the landscape, which are indicated on a map of the main locations and parishes at the end of the chapter. They were encountered by the author in a variety of contexts from family memories to schoolyard 'scarers' and pub anecdotes. Some tale types are relatively well referenced in works such as those by Katherine Briggs,[23] or parallel a tale with a location elsewhere in Cornwall in the Bottrell or Hunt collections. Others are not so well known. The cultural context will be considered in the conclusion.

Dando or Dondo

Location: St Germans, Sheviock (Prior's Brake and Georges lane), Erth, river Lynher (Dandy Hole), the cliffs between Rame and Downderry, Horsepool lane, Eglaroose, Lantic, St Winnols.

Summary: Legend of the Wild Hunt type. A dissolute priest (in one version Dando) and his companions break the Sabbath to go hunting and feasting. The priest and his hounds become separated from the main party while chasing a fine stag. He comes across a sumptuous feast in a woodland glade and a dark stranger (the Dondo) offers hospitality. The greedy priest eats and drinks his fill. When challenged by the stranger over ownership of the game he says if he could 'find food and drink again as good as that which he had just tasted on Erth (pun on the location) then he would ride to Hell and back to find it'. The stranger says 'Then so you shall!'. He turns into a horned beast (the Dondo or Old Nic) and pursues the priest with his own pack. A wild hunt ensues covering a number of parishes until the priest and his hounds leap into the river Lynher (a spot still known as the Dandy Hole) and disappear, followed by the Devil's hunt. Between Halloween and early February the wild hunt may be heard on stormy nights particularly before shipwrecks, hunting the souls of the recently deceased, sometimes disappearing into the cliffs beside the Brawn and the Long Stone near Downderry. The living caught up in the wild hunt may only survive if they close their eyes, pray and keep faith in god. They will be set down unharmed where they were first swept up, though the hair on their heads may well have turned white. Sometimes the Dondo's wagon is heard rattling along the lanes carrying the dead and picking up the odd foolish traveller along the way.[24]

King of the Cormorants

Location: Erth, Ince Castle, river Lynher (Dandy Hole), Sheviock woods, Polbathic and St Germans

Summary: This legend is a conflation of an historical legend concerning Henry Killigrew, the Royalist MP for Looe during the Civil War, who built Ince Castle and a version of the British Bluebeard tale, Mr Fox. The historical Killigrew is reputed to have had four wives at the same time. A mysterious stranger, Henry Killigrew, buys some bog and waste-land from a greedy local landowner (sometimes referred to as lord of Erth Manor) to build a castle. The landowner demands an excessive sum of gold and silver for a lease (with three lives) and rather than get anything less promises the stranger he can keep the castle as long as he marries and remains married to one of his four daughters. The agreement is sealed. To the landowner's surprise in no time at all a magnificent house, Ince Castle, is built as if by magic and servants installed. The castle has four towers, one on each corner but the towers have no windows. A great banquet and ball take place for all the gentry at which the stranger chooses the eldest daughter as his bride. The wedding, not very grand in contrast to the ball, takes place almost immediately, but within a short period of time the landowner is shocked to receive a message that his daughter has died and the stranger demands according to the agreement the second daughter as his wife. The same sequence of events occur with the second and third daughters until the lord of the manor is faced only nine months after marrying off his first daughter with losing his last, youngest and favourite child. Despite his pleas and promise to return the gold and silver the stranger will not relent and takes the youngest as well.

Unknown to anyone Killigrew has imprisoned a bride in each tower of the castle. The first bride gives birth to a child, but before he can butcher them both the delivery of a lost letter by a postman, addressed to the first wife but delivered to the youngest, reveals the true situation. The resourceful youngest daughter escapes and raises the alarm. The lord of the manor and an angry crowd attack the castle and release the imprisoned brides. Killigrew tries to escape but is cornered and changes into a large black bird, apparently a cormorant given the reference to the 'mankin' tree where cormorants roost. He is spotted in a big 'mankin' tree with other cormorants beside the river Lynher and is shot through the heart. The bird with a terrible scream dives with all his family into the Dandy Hole.

The historical Killigrew, despite his local unpopularity, seems to have escaped to London where he became a favourite of the king and continued as dissolute as ever plotting to gain the property of honest folk. As proof of the tale it was claimed the old coat of arms of the Killigrews, left at Ince but now lost, showed the strange, large black bird with its outstretched wings.[25]

Finnygook

Location: Portwrinkle, Trewrickle, Crafthole, Whitsand Bay, Cawsand, Mew Stone, Lammana or Looe Island

Summary: A famous smuggler called Silas Finn or Finny operated between the Mew Stone and Looe Island and often landed his goods at Portwrinkle. One night he was caught by the excise men and rather than take his punishment agreed to lure the other local smugglers into a cove (still called Finnygook beach) where the excise men could catch them. So that he would not be recognised or caught again he disguised himself as a woman in a bonnet. He stood on the cliffs, waving a lantern until the smugglers landed and were caught, at which point he fled. The ghost of Finny is said to haunt the cliffs around Portwrinkle and Crafthole unable to lie at rest because of his treachery. There was always local disagreement as to whether the 'gook' in Finnygook was originally a Cornish word for his ghost, his cove, or the lady's bonnet. Whether he was related to the famous Finn and Hooper families, which included the legendary black, female smuggler, Joan Finn of Looe Island is also a matter of speculation. The public house at Crafthole is still called the Finnygook, while in Looe Guildhall there is a painting by John Robertson Reid, described as 'Arrest of a Smuggler', depicting the arrest of Amram Hooper who with his sister Jochabed were connected with smuggling at Looe Island. An interesting element is the figure of the negress in the background of the painting, presumably being a representation of Joan Finn.[26]

Patten Peg

Location: Antony, St John, Wolsdon, Lower Tregantle, Trelay farm

Summary: This tale of a witch is referred to in Hunt. The location is Antony church steps cottages and the older row of cottages on the opposite side of the road that were demolished in the Second World War. The version still in circulation in the 1950s was known as Patten Peg, rather than Miss Alsey, as given in Hunt. It focuses on the ghostly clatter of the patten shoes coming down the church steps as the old woman continues her walk from Trelay farm, through the cemetery to the old cottage. This was sometimes re-told by adolescents to terrify younger children and send them home at night and if possible it was accompanied by someone hidden away, providing a sudden clattering noise. The witch was rumoured to have ill wished someone at Trelay Farm who refused her a cup of milk. When the unfortunate individual died and was buried she went at night into Antony Church cemetery and cut the thigh off the corpse. She used the flesh for a roast and put the rest in a stew. Later she uses a toad, an 'athercob' (cob appears to be a dialect word for a type of spider) and the 'ground up' thigh bones in casting her spells. Hence after her death she spent her time as an unquiet soul roaming the churchyard and her old haunts trying to find the grave of her victim to make amends. Hunt deals with her ability to 'go into a toad', some kind of familiar spirit, and do evil to those she had cursed. Eventually the toad is caught and badly burnt, later the old woman is found dead in her cottage bearing the same burn marks as the toad. This is seen as certain proof of her witchcraft. An interesting undercurrent to the tale is the old woman's poverty and her inability or refusal to pay the rent to her landlord, which also leads to a curse on his family.[27]

Blighberry or Blackberry Round

Location: Antony, St John Mill, Wolsdon House, Ringdon field ('barrow')

Summary: I believe this has a literary origin perhaps in one of the almanacs or collections because of the obvious folktale motifs it includes. I have summarised the basic plot from childhood memory, without the more literary repetitions in the telling. What is of interest is the way this has been applied to local landscape features such as the rumoured ancient barrow in Ringdon field, behind Wolsdon House, once known as Blighberry or Blackberry round. If it does derive from an authentic local tradition it may be significant, given the role of the fierce black dogs in the tale, that one derivation for Wolsdon is believed to be the old English Wolf's Hill. A miller at St John mill finds that the flour he has ground is being stolen at night by three old women; they squeeze under the mill door in the form of toads. Before he can intervene they are chased away by three black hounds with fiery eyes. He follows the hounds until they disappear into Blighberry round. (Repetition of the events in the mill over three Fridays or three full moons etc, he sees three dogs go into the mound and three men come out, etc). The miller leaving his family armed but safe in the millhouse is able to follow the hounds on the final night and goes into the mound where he discovers a hoard of treasure. He rushes home to his wife and family but when he tries to tell them what he has discovered they recoil in terror and he is shot dead. He had not realised that he had turned into a fierce black hound whose voice when he tried to speak was heard instead as an 'eery howling'; a sound which may still frighten those walking from Antony to St John through the woods late at night.[28]

Lady Mount Edgecombe's Ring

Location: Cremyll, Maker Church, Mount Edgecombe, St Julian's Well

Summary: One of the Edgecombes took a young wife (his cousin?) and was married in Maker church before returning to Mount Edgecombe house. On the bridal night the bride swooned away into a sleep from which she could not be woken. So deep was the sleep she was barely breathing. Despite trying a number of remedies no one could wake her. As a last resort a flask of water was brought from St Julian's well by the lord's manservant and this was thrown over the sleeping bride who promptly recovered. The happy couple went on honeymoon but when they returned and spent their first night back in the house the bride again went into a deep sleep. Edgecombe sent his manservant to run again to the saint's well and fetch the water needed to revive his wife. (It was stressed that the 'hind' or manservant had previously been a skinner or a tanner! This odd detail about an unpleasant occupation may be a rather sly allusion to families with these surnames who used to live in the locality).

Once again the cure worked and she recovered. Within a few more weeks the young wife announced one evening that she was pregnant, but scarcely had she uttered the words than she again went into a deep death-like trance. The manservant was sent to the well again, but being too lazy to run all the way there he filled the flask instead from the pump behind the house. When the water was thrown on the sleeping Lady Mount Edgecombe she failed to awaken. The servant terrified he would be found out said nothing. After everything else failed and there was no trace of the faintest breath in her body, the husband was forced sorrowfully to bury his wife in the family vault. She was entombed in her bridal gown with all her jewellery. This was too much for the rascally manservant who bided his time and late one night broke into the vault to steal the jewels. Lady Mount Edgecombe had a fine diamond wedding ring on her finger but try as he might he could not get it off. Sharpening his knife with a little water and a whetstone he began to cut through her finger. Whereupon she woke with a tremendous start and screamed out so loud the house servants and her husband were aroused and came to the vault. The terrified manservant ran off to West Stonehouse (Millbrook) and was never seen again, despite the offer of a reward by the grateful Lord Edgecombe, who had recovered not just his wife but his unborn child as well.[29]

Telling Tales in Familiar Landscapes

All of the legends above have an implicit moral centre in the attribution of praise or blame to the actions of the protagonists. Even the most archaic such as the Dondo demand a familiarity with certain landscape features. There is a shared experience established through the narrative event; the relation of tale-teller and audience, to the narrated event, however distant in the past this might be. Only in transcription are such tales frozen in time, in reality they evolve, disappear and may indeed be rediscovered. Folklore is continually and creatively reinvented and is an aspect of a community's ability to stabilise an identity around a set of common or customary cultural practices. Where the community is a relatively settled one, or at least imagines itself to be so, folkloric creativity involves claims on specific locations in the imagined landscape.

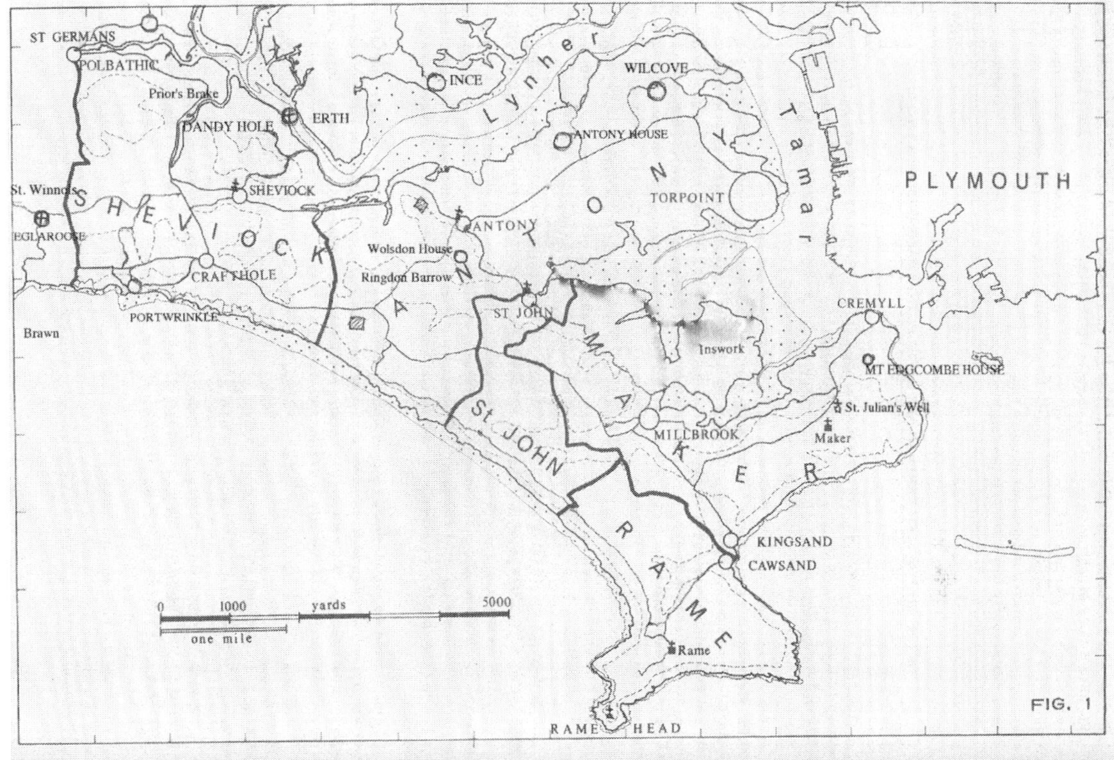

Map of the Rame peninsula

In a fascinating recent study by Michael Wilson, the ways in which children and young people adapted urban legends to their own experiences demonstrates this continuing cultural creativity.[30] Wilson's research which involved fieldwork in Devon and Cornwall as well as in Ireland, focused in part on the rapid transmission and adaptation locally of the 'Mad Axeman' stories from the 1960s (based on an actual criminal, Frank Mitchell, who had escaped from Dartmoor Prison). These rapidly developed into modern urban legends featuring a homicidal maniac as reflected in tales like 'The Hook' and 'The Licked Hand'. Never found alive despite a massive police hunt, it was believed that the real Mitchell went to London but was there murdered by the Kray twins, figures who themselves were well on the way to becoming criminal legends that would haunt popular consciousness. Local allusions to this type of legacy, which might appear impenetrable to an outsider, often crop up in humorous or sarcastic asides linking families or individuals to a past event. These were famously referred to as 'having a dig' at someone or something that the community might agree was of dubious worth or honesty. Recent examples would be anecdotes attached to a famous local Liberal MP elected amongst an outburst of non-conformist radicalism to the Bodmin constituency in the 1960s,[31] whose campaign was described by a disgruntled opponent as having 'more glamour than the fairies', i.e. a complete illusion. The same MP was more or less forced out of the seat later in relation to the collapse of a commercial venture brought over from the USA, known as 'The Welcome Wagon'. One anonymous wag immediately described the Welcome Wagon venture as 'decked out like the Dondo's wagon', very easy and attractive to get into, but damn near impossible to get out of!'

So alongside horror and hauntings a whole sub-genre of comical or foolish tales invites the local audience, who 'knew' the characters involved, to participate in forms of public ridicule. In this context the author has come across a series of 'real' local events and 'characters' well on the way to becoming local legends in their community, including themes such as 'Buried at Sea', 'The Corpse that crossed the Tamar', the 'Blind Driver' and 'My Best Suit', which involve local families, funerals, corpses, undertakers, eccentric vicars and the police. Ghost stories and hauntings continue to have their appeal and unusually seem to completely bridge the normal barriers of class and status.[32] Indeed, the persistence of ghosts in Cornwall may relate much more directly than elsewhere to the hold of Methodism, reflecting Wesley's own well-known views on this subject.[33]

The 'genii locii' then have proved surprisingly difficult to evict from the landscape. The fact that local folklore has continued and has been replenished by later generations indicates its continuing function for the community rather than its significance as a survival. It is perhaps not so surprising that traditional tales coexist with modern adaptations and that innovation is an important part of the folklore legacy of the locality. In some cases, as Wilson's study has found tales have been brought up to date in ways that show the influence of horror films and pulp fiction; what contemporary folklorists would consider to be the transmission of urban legends.[34] Given the universal aspect of folklore motifs,[35] why do these new legends still require a specific locality and landscape for the community? Part of the answer lies with what Labov identified in his work on narratives of personal experience as the rules that govern narrative preconstruction.[36] By way of the human faculty for story-telling 'real' local events and individuals become transformed by the devices of narrative and with the passage of time can be 'folklorised' into more universal functions of what may become a recognizable 'tale type'? Another aspect of this process is to be found in the social psychology of stories which imply a common history and set of experiences. Also important is the way in which participation in such forms of common knowledge provides the framework of a collective identity which excludes those from outside; those who 'do not know' the relations that bind the community together, even where these remembered relations include family feuds, hostility and inherited resentments.

Conclusion

For the relatively impoverished fishing and farming community of Portwrinkle and the surrounding villages in the nineteenth century the economic reality had been that of the land or the harbour. However, although the gentry and the wealthy might own most of the land or even the fishing nets, the labourers that lived and worked on it possessed it in other ways. A common conviction was that those who worked the land were those that really shaped the landscape and had rights in it. Those who were born and bred in a place, married and raised their families and eventually died and were buried there had claims to its possession and knew its history. The respectable aristocracy might occupy the most impressive tombs in the church but the cemeteries and lanes were crowded with the ghosts of other remembered family members and legendary figures: Finny the notorious smuggler; Killigrew, the murderous, bigamist aristocrat; Lady Mount Edgecombe, the enchanted wife; Dando the dissolute priest of the 'old corrupt established church'. In England the myth of the Norman Yoke has had a long history reflecting, like tales of Robin Hood, the resentment of common folk against poverty and injustice.[37] In Cornwall this tradition had a unique twist in that resentment was rather against the Saxon Yoke and contrasted with 'good King Arthur's days'.[38] One aspect of this assertion of an 'unofficial' or unrecognised historic identity is the social and psychological possession of the landscape and the folk wisdom that the classical folklorists from the Grimm brothers onwards believed they had discovered in common folk. Respectable and literate members of the labouring class had found in the published collections of the folklorists a kind of history, which was no longer just of monarchs and empires. The national character it seemed was reflected in the character of the folk, but this character itself depended on the 'little' histories of particular communities, localities and ethnic groups.

Even today the lone visitor walking the coastal path between Rame Head and Looe Island, particularly on a late winter's evening, despite the impressive coastal landscape might be forgiven the odd moment of anxiety and disquiet at the lack of fellow human company. Would the lonely traveller be more at ease or less so, if he was aware that the landscape through which he was making his way was crowded with so many ghosts and spectres! Every landscape has its story to tell and often more than one.

Notes

1. Kent C Ryden, *Mapping the Invisible Landscape: Folklore, Writing and Sense of Place*, University of Iowa Press, 1993, p 286.
2. J Barrell, *The Dark Side of the Landscape: the Rural Poor in English Painting, 1730-1840*, Cambridge University Press, 1980, pp. 6-13
3. Diarmaid O' Giolla in, *Locating Irish Folklore: Tradition, Modernity, Identity*, Cork, 2000, pp. 32-33; George D Zimmerman, *The Irish Storyteller*, Four Courts Press, 2001. See also Michael Wilson, *Performance and Practice: Oral Narrative Traditions and Teenagers in Britain and Ireland*, Ashgate, 1997, pp. 3-9
4. Robert Keys, 'The Family Album: The Role of the Visual in Oral History and the Cultural Context of the Photograph in Recovering Memory' in Garry Tregidga (ed.), *Narratives of the Family: Kinship and Identity in Cornwall*, Kresenn Kernow, 2009, pp. 21-38.
5. James Vernon, 'Border Crossings: Cornwall and the English Imagination' in Geoffrey Cubitt (ed.), *Imagining Nations*, Manchester University Press, 1998, p 96 see also R Perry, 'The Changing Face of Celtic Tourism in Cornwall, 1875-1975' in P Payton (ed), *Cornish Studies: Seven*, University of Exeter Press, 1999, pp. 94-106.
6. Tony Carne, *Cornwall's Forgotten Corner*, Lodenek Press, 1986.
7. Keys, 'The Family Album' in Tregidga (ed.), *Narratives of the Family*, 2009, pp. 21-38.
8. Bernard Deacon, *A Concise History of Cornwall*, University of Wales Press, 2007, pp 159-60; Tony Deane and Tony Shaw, *Folkore of Cornwall*, 2003 edition, p 25ff
9. Robert Hunt, *Popular Romances of the West of England or The Drolls, Traditions and Superstitions of Old Cornwall*, Chatto & Windus, 1903 edition; William Bottrell, *Traditions and Hearthside Stories of West Cornwall in Two Volumes*, Vol. 1, 1870 and Vol. 2, 1873, Beare & Son
10. E P Thompson, *Customs in Common: Studies in Traditional Popular Culture*, Merlin Press, 1991, pp. 40-48 and 467-530, See also Paul Robinson, 'Royal Justice and Folk Justice: Conflict over a Skimmington in Polterne, 1857' in *Wiltshire Archaeological and Natural History Magazine*, N83, 1990, pp 147-53; R A Jones, 'Popular Culture, Policing and the Dissappearance of the Caffyl Pren in Cardigan, 1837-50', in *Ceredigion*, N11, 1998-99, pp. 193-9.
11. Silvia Pieroni, 'Antonio Gramsci e il folklore: i contributi gramsciani allo sviluppo dell'antropologia italiana attraverso Lettere e Quaderni', in *Antrocom*, 2005, Vol 1, N,2, pp.187-88 and Antonio Gramsci, *Selections from Cultural Writings*, Lawrence & Wishart, 1985, p. 189 and p. 421
12. George Ewart Evans, *Ask the Fellows who Cut the Hay*, Faber & Faber, 1956; *The Pattern under the Plough: Aspects of the Folk*

Life of East Anglia, Faber & Faber, 1966 ; *Where Beards Wag All: the relevance of Oral Tradition*, Faber & Faber, 1972.

13. Keys, 'The Family Album' in Tregidga (ed.), *Narratives of the Family*, 2009, pp. 21-38.
14. Linda Degh, *Legend and Belief: Dialectics of a folklore genre*, University of Indiana Press, 2001, pp 41-2 and p 69; see also Linda Degh and Andrew Vazsonyi, 'The Memorate and the Fabulate' in *Journal of American Folklore*, Vol 87,N 345, 1974, pp 225-39 and Larry Danielson, 'Towards the Analysis of Vernacular Texts: The Supernatural Narrative in Oral and Popular Print Sources', in *Journal of the Folklore Institute*, Vol 16, N 3, 1979, pp 130-154.
15. Gramsci, opp cit p189
16. Vladimir Propp, *Morphology of the Folktale*, 2nd edition (ed) L Wagner trans L Scott, University of Texas Press, 1975; V Propp, *Theory and History of Folklore*, University of Minnesota Press,1984 and Robert Keys , 'Morphology of the Cornish Folktale', paper given to the Cornish Audio-Visual Archive (CAVA) at Institute of Cornish Studies, 2009.
17. Garry Tregidga, 'The Politics of the Celto-Cornish Revival, 1886-1939', pp.125-50; Ronald Perry, 'Celtic Revival and economic development in Edwardian Cornwall', pp112-24; David Everett, 'Celtic Revival and the Anglican Church in Cornwall'; all in P Payton (ed.) *Cornish Studies: Five*, University of Exeter Press, 1997.
18. Raymond Williams, *The Country and the City*, Oxford University Press, 1973, pp. 13-33 & 96-108.
19. Katherine M Briggs, *A Dictionary of British Folktales in the English Language* (4 Volumes), University of Indiana Press, 1971; *An Encyclopedia of Fairies*, Penquin, 1976.
20. Deacon, opp cit pp.159-60.
21. *Doidges Western Counties Illustrated Annual*, Hoyten & Cole, 1911, pp 320-347.
22. Benedict Andersen, *Imagined Communities: Reflecting on the Origin and Spread of Nationalism*, Verso, 1983, pp. 4-7; for a critical review, Radikhai Desai, 'The Inadvertence of Benedict Anderson: Engaging Imagined Communities, pp 1-19 at http://japanfocus.org and Eric Hobsbaum & Terence Ranger (eds.), *The Invention of Tradition*, Cambridge University Press, 1983.
23. Briggs, opp cit, pp. 436-7 and K M Briggs, *The Fairies in English Tradition and Literature*, University of Chicago Press, 1967, pp. 49-51; see also C Lindahl, J McNamara & J Lindow (eds.) *Medieval Folklore: A Guide to Myths, Legends, Tales, Beliefs and Customs*, Oxford University Press, 2002, p. 432.
24. Robert Hunt, first series, loc cit pp 241-44 and pp 251-2 see also second series, loc cit p 402 for 'mock mayor at St Germans on Oak Apple day, 29 May which involved ecclesiastical mockery and parade with a decorated wagon ; T Quiller Couch, *The Folklore of a Cornish Village*, 1855 and 1857, included in J Quiller Couch, *History of Polperro*, 1871 for a variant of the Dando story; G A Kempthorne, *History of Sheviock*, Begg, Kennedy and Elder, 1934, for speculation on the origin of the name Dando and the context of the events; there is a depiction of a huntsman with his dog on a Miserere in St Germans Church, reputed to be Dando, see J. E Spence, *A short history and guide to the Church of St Germans*, 1973, p. 11
25. Sir Charles Oman, 'Castles', *Great Western Railways*, 1926, pp. 108-9.
26. Michael Dunn, *The Looe Island Story*, Polperro Heritage Press, 2005, pp. 54-58.
27. Hunt, loc cit for 'Witch and Toad', second series, pp. 337-9
28. Robert Keys, from family members in 1950s.
29. Robert Keys, from family members in the 1950s.
30. Wilson, loc cit, pp. 41-48 and pp 69-86; see also Jack Zipes, *Breaking the Magic Spell: Radical Theories of Folk and Fairy Tales*, Routledge, 1992.
31. Garry Tregidga, 'Bodmin Man: Peter Bessell and Cornish Politics in the 1950s and 1960s' in Philip Payton (ed.), *Cornish Studies: Eight*, University of Exeter Press, 2000, pp. 161-81.
32. Paul White, *Classic Westcountry Ghost Stories*, Tor Mark Press, pp.14-16, for the Antony death-bed visitor as recorded in a letter by Lady Pole-Carew in December, 1883
33. Owen Davies, *Witchcraft, Magic and Culture, 1736-1951*, Manchester University Press, 1999 , pp. 118-125.
34. Wilson, loc cit pp 87-90 and Paul Smith (ed.), *Perspectives on Contemporary Legend*, CECTAL, 1984.
35. Alan Dundes *(ed.), The Study of Folklore*, Prentice-Hall, 1965; Stith Thompson, *The Folktale*, University of California Press, 1977.
36. William Labov, 'Oral Narratives of Personal Experience', in *Cambridge Encyclopedia of the Language Sciences*, Jan 2011 and W Labov,' Narrative Pre-construction' in *Narrative Inquiry*, 16, pp. 37-45 for an analysis of the evaluative effect of inserting ordinary events into narrative.
37. Maurice Keen, *The Outlaws of Medieval Legend*, Routledge, Keegan &Paul,1987 edition, pp xvi-xix; where the author points out that the gentry rather than the common people were the protagonists of most 'outlaw' Ballads; see J C Holt, *Robin Hood*, Thames & Hudson, 1984, pp.7-13 for the definitive examination of the legend.
38. Simon Tresize, 'The Celt, the Saxon and the Cornishman: stereotypes and counter-stereotypes of the Victorian period' in Philip Payton (ed.), *Cornish Studies: Eight*, University of Exeter Press, 2000, pp. 54-6.

Changing landscapes: Oral history and the market gardening communities of the Tamar Valley

Kay Milden

'Now the Valley has gone back to how it was before I even knew it. The hills back to growing trees – they'd been cleared by the miners in the depression – now it's all back to the trees growing again.'[1]

Introduction

Since 2002 the Cornish Audio Visual Archive (CAVA), the Tamar Valley AONB and the National Trust have worked in conjunction to create a history of the horticultural industry in the Tamar Valley. A series of oral history interviews were recorded with retired market gardeners as well as horticulturalists currently working in the Tamar Valley. This article will explore the ways that the local inhabitants respond to the changes in the surrounding environment and how this landscape is interwoven within the oral tradition of the Tamar Valley's market gardening communities. Oral history has the unique ability to span time dimensions, explore the intricacies of spatial identity, and to 'give voice' to community histories that may otherwise be unheard. Developments in Cornish Studies over the last decade have begun to move on from 'macro-level' perspectives and have begun to analyse the complexities of Cornish identity at the 'micro-peripheral' level of the sub-regions such as the Tamar Valley.[2] Moreover, the Tamar Valley forms part of the Cornwall-Devon borderlands; therefore, the historical dynamics between the two 'halves' of the Tamar Valley will also be considered.

Harvesting memories in the Tamar Valley

Oral history has begun to produce multifaceted benefits in the research of the market gardening industry and landscape heritage of the Tamar Valley. On a practical level, oral history recordings have played a part in conserving the precious knowledge of traditional horticultural skills and plant varieties unique to the Tamar Valley. Who better to ask than the people who actually worked the land in the Valley to create a record of how local crops were cultivated, how old tools were used, how pests and diseases were treated, and how the produce was transported? Through interviewing people who were involved in market gardening, oral history also provides a personal account of each individual's struggle to survive the dominance of the 'global market' and mass farming techniques, which has arguably been greatly responsible for the virtual disappearance of the market gardening industry in the Tamar Valley. Interviewing both retired and current horticulturists has proven to be very enlightening and at times very moving experience, revealing the layers of each person's individual life story and their emotional struggle of working with the land, in a way that could not be replicated through conventional textual historical sources. The Veale family are one of the last remaining market gardening businesses in the St Dominick Parish. Gerald Veale related the struggles now facing his own business and other local growers in the Valley:

> The markets up-country are not so plentiful as they were ten year ago – we only had one this week went out of business – there's less people for us to send to. Of course, you get all this foreign stuff now from Italy, France and Spain ... so you've got that to contend with as well. [...] It's mostly family concerns in this area, you can't get no outside labour ...well I don't blame them really, because it's out in all weathers.[3]

The impact that the global market has had on local growers is clear from this extract. Shortages in labour power have also made it tougher for some market gardeners to keep going. Arguably this problem began at the local level in the years after the Second World War when the developments of improved transport links and indoor employment in Plymouth factories and Devonport Dockyard proved financially and physically less stressful than labouring on the land. Of course, every individual has experienced the economic and social transformation within local horticulture in varying degrees and chronologies.

Oral testimony has provided a wide spectrum of historical versions for the reason why the decline of the market gardening industry took place. Some individuals perceive the Second World War as being the turning point in the gradual decline in the industry, due to the younger generation returning home from military service and deciding that they didn't want to return to the 'hard toil' of working on the land, and therefore looked for alternative employment with better pay and working conditions . Others believe that the market gardening industry actually reached an all-time peak after the War, due to a generation of younger men returning from War and wishing to set up their own market gardens when they came home; this was coupled with a revival of the local Plymouth markets due to the rebuilding of the city after the Blitz. The third narrative is that the War, apart from certain restrictions on crops, made no real impact on local horticulture and things generally 'went on as before', and the gradual decline came in the 1960s due to changes in transport and labour shortages. None of these timescales or explanations is wrong; they merely demonstrate the diverse multiplicity in individual experience of socio-economic change which occurred within the Tamar Valley. Indeed, oral history used to be criticised for the bias and unreliability of using

memory as a historical source. Since the 1970s however, revisionist oral historians emphasised the unique quality inherent in the genre, and so called 'discrepancies' or 'contradictions' within oral testimony are now valued as relevant historical evidence.[4]

A Celtic or a Kinship Border?

Oral history provides the theoretical freedom to explore the intricacies of spatial identity at the level of locality. Indeed, the Tamar Valley's unique landscape heritage and geographic position spanning the Cornwall-Devon border demand in-depth research in its own right.

Athelstan set the Tamar as the border between England and Cornwall in the year 936. Hitherto the river has historically been perceived by many as the border not just between two counties, but the frontier between 'Anglo-Devon' and 'Celtic Cornwall'. Indeed, it could be argued that Cornwall developed a 'dual identity', the tension between it existing as both 'Celtic country' and 'English county' (or at least an English Duchy), continuing into its modern history. Borders, however, are not just physical entities, they are also human constructions. What is more, it is not just the geographical and political dimensions of borders that can change over time; peoples' relationship with borders can also go through a number of transformations. The workings of both spatial and cultural identity are much more complex than at first glance when we consider, in Anthony Cohen's words, the existence of 'mental borders'. Cohen argued that borders are a 'psychological' as well as a geographical phenomenon, that can shift according to the time, place and culture that each individual finds him or herself encompassed within.[5] Cohen's theory regarding mental borders is no less relevant to the complex nature of spatial identity within the rural hinterlands of the Tamar Valley.

Due to current government proposals to create a new cross-border constituency, the Tamar's history as an ethno-political border has recently come under the spotlight once again. The proposals have aroused much criticism for showing a lack of respect and understanding to Cornwall's cultural, political and economic distinctiveness. David Cameron added heat to the debate by allegedly making a 'gaffe' moments before a television interview, commenting that, 'It's the Tamar, not the Amazon, for Heaven's sake'[5] Contemporary concerns over the encroachment of England into Cornish territory in many ways echo events occurring over thirty years ago. The South East Cornwall region as a whole, found itself at the heart of a political mêlée during the 1960s and 1970s. Fears over the 'Devon Wall' reforms (which merged many of Cornwall's public services with Devon) and plans for a 'Tamarside county' swallowing South East

Gerald Veale, a market gardener from the Cornish parish of St Dominick (Photograph copyright of Ted Giffords (2003) and courtesy of Tamar Vallley AONB)

Cornwall into the governmental control of Plymouth City Council, promoted the Tamar's importance as a fortress to protect Cornish autonomy.[6] A programme made for regional television in 1973 demonstrates that many Cornish inhabitants of the Tamar Valley regarded the river as the geographic and cultural boundary separating them from the English on the Devon side.[7] Moreover, just over a decade before this film was made the Tamar Road Bridge was opened, creating faster and more accessible transportation links between the two sides of the river. This concern is voiced in the film by a number of participants. One interviewee from Gunnislake referred to the days of King Athelstan, and asserted that his declaration of the Tamar as the border in the tenth century was still law, meaning that officially Cornwall was still part of 'West Wales.'[8]

Nonetheless, a 'Celtic-English border' is just one of the Tamar's guises. There is evidence to suggest that for many living in this part of the Cornish borderland, the river is remembered as a corridor that fostered trade and kinship ties across the Tamar. Although there may well exist a sense of 'unconscious difference' between the opposite sides of the river, in many parts of the Valley the landscape is similar. The people have also been linked by the industry reaped from its natural resources and consequently by the migration of people across the border for purposes of employment. Market gardening, mining and other local industries inextricably bound-up with the Tamar Valley's landscape has nurtured cross-border kinship and trade ties that make the boundaries between the Cornwall and Devon side of the river less palpable than in 'frontier towns' such as Saltash.[9] The existence of this 'kinship border' is suggested from an extract of an interview with Iris Snell, who comes from a family of market gardeners on the Devon side of the river at South Ward Farm. She remarked that 'There was always rivalry between Dad's side of the river, over Ward and over St Dominick ... When they picked cherries, Dad said they used to shout across the river from one cherry tree to the other, across the river, right up through'.[10]

When asked if there was a sense of difference between the Cornish and Devonian sides of the river, Iris replied that there didn't exist any strong feeling of difference from the opposite sides, only a 'friendly rivalry' between the growers as to whose crops would produce earliest. It would seem that the work and kinship networks also produced as much unity as separation; Iris's own family history demonstrates this point. Through patterns of cross-border marriage and migration, she has family connections on both sides of the Tamar. The paternal side of her family came from the Cornish half of the border and the maternal side from the Devon side. Iris herself was born on the Devon side of the Tamar and married a Cornishman, John Snell, who was born at Gunnislake; the couple now reside on the Devon side at Bere Alston. It is interesting to note that although her father was born and raised at St Dominick, on the Cornish side of the border, Iris refers to the Devon side as 'Dad's side of the river.' This suggests that spatial identity can shift according to ownership of land, homestead and marriage; often overriding one's place of birth. Just as the landscape can alter over time or through different seasons, likewise peoples 'sense of place' go through stages of metamorphosis. Certainly it would seem for many individuals involved on the horticulture in its heyday in the Tamar Valley, there may have been an unconscious sense of difference or 'rivalry' between the opposing 'geographic' sides of the Tamar, but the unity necessitated by industry and kinship networks certainly blurred the 'mental' borders between the two areas.

By the 1970s, however, much of the Valley's horticultural landscape, and the traditional 'way of life' associated with it, was under threat. The market gardening industry was in decline and consequently the landscape was changing, either reverting back to woodland or scrubland and traditional crops being replaced by more profitable ventures. The next generation of horticulturalists found it increasingly difficult to carry on the family business and began to find better paid work in factories and shops in Plymouth or in Devonport Dockyard. Both the physical and human construct of the landscape has undergone considerable change in recent decades. Within the oral tradition of the Tamar Valley, there is a collective narrative of the surrounding landscape revolving a 'full circle'. As will now be discussed, the concept of the cyclical process of nature, not only serve to make sense of the environmental changes that have occurred throughout much of the Tamar Valley, but also the socio-economic and cultural transitions as well.

Full Circle: Landscape Heritage in the Tamar Valley

During recent decades the decline of the market gardening industry has not only transformed the social and economic life of the Valley, but the landscape and the way in which local people 'perceive' their surrounding environment has similarly evolved. In the space of around a hundred years the landscape changed from wooded valley slopes to a patchwork of small market gardens coinciding with the rise of the industry, and then consequently reverted to trees and scrubland after the demise of the industry. One of the most prominent factors in the narratives of market gardeners is the impact of the changing landscape over the last century. Such 'lifescape' narratives, often interweave the story of the Tamar Valley's landscape with the life stories of the communities that inhabit this hinterland. The vacillation between mankind and nature is not surprisingly even more relevant to agricultural and horticultural workers, whose socio-economic existence has been inevitably bound with the forces of Mother Earth. For many retired horticultural workers in the Tamar Valley, the pattern of the landscape cycle revolving 'from nature to human then back to nature' has almost become a 'collective memory'[11] Even more fascinating however, was that many interviewees seemed to interweave the stages of their own lives within the 'life cycle' of the changing landscape surrounding them. Denis Cosgrove has drawn attention to the correlation between the cycles of nature and human existence:

> The cyclical patterns of nature: seasonal weather, the recurrence in plant and animal life, of birth, death and rebirth, are enduring. They are a dimension of the life experience of each human individual and every human society. It is not difficult to appreciate how human life processes are read into those of the natural world, for they are in large measure the same and afford a means of expressing an unalienated relationship with the physical milieu.[12]

Of course, part of the beauty of oral history is that it considers the perspectives and experience of the individual, and not just structured social groups. Although collective

or community narratives do exist with the Tamar Valley, as discussed, they inevitably differ in character and emphasis according to the current political and socio-cultural backdrop. Moreover landscapes are not merely 'seen', but they are internally experienced, emotionally constructed and expressed through the 'social makeup' of each individual. Cosgove expands on this concept by saying that 'Landscape denotes the external world mediated through subjective human experience in a way that neither region nor area immediately suggest. Landscape is not merely the world we see; it is a construction, a composition of that world'.[13]

D.W. Meinig argues that different people perceive surroundings through different 'landscape concepts'. Two of these concepts are: 'landscape as nature'; for this perceiver all the works of man are paltry and temporal compared to the fundamental presence of nature. Others will see 'landscape as habitat'; whereby every landscape is a home for mankind, which works with nature, creating resources out of nature's materials: 'in short man domesticating the earth'.[14] But it is often a *tension* between these two views that is apparent in many of the narratives from horticulturalists in the Tamar Valley. This landscape 'tension' has, in part, created this collective oral tradition in certain communities, of nature revolving a 'full circle'. Of course, this is not unique to the Tamar Valley; even throughout modern society we are all still responsive to the cycle of nature: the feeling we get from different environments or landscapes, the physical and mental effects of the changing seasons and weather. But the presence of nature in the lives of horticulturalists in the Tamar Valley has been an intrinsic part of their existence: working outdoors in all weathers, trying to tame the elements, while at the same time working with nature in order to make a living. Many individuals have recalled the physical and mental distress that was involved in the horticultural trade: long hours, hard toil and whole crops could be devastated by bad weather or disease. But at the same time, despite the pain and heartache that working the Valley's landscape could inflict, there is almost a sense of sadness and lament for a *way of life* that has been lost with the demise of the market gardening industry.[15]

Iris Snell, a Cornish-Devonian (Photograph copyright of Ted Giffords (2003) and courtesy of Tamar Vallley AONB)

Patrick Laviolette has drawn attention to the 'clashing' images of Cornwall's landscape; images of the 'deathliness' of Cornwall's historic landscape stand in competition to images of regeneration connected to tourism and cultural revival. Expanding on this theme, Laviolette argues that the 'diffuse sense of deathliness' actually creates a 'solidarity' between communities, relating back to 'dying-out ways of life' that lay dormant within Cornwall's landscape.[16] Similarly in the Tamar Valley, opposing images of death and regeneration exist. Overgrown mine engine houses and market gardens, derelict packing sheds, have been 'taken back by nature', and the area is now looking towards tourism and recreation as a new means of sustainability. The concept of full circle unites the local community in 'solidarity'; the memories of the market gardens that *now lay at rest* under the trees and undergrowth almost seem to represent the *death* of their community as it was when the gardens were *alive*. Whatever 'truths' are revealed by the concept of the Tamar Valley's full circle, it is a narrative that not only serves to understand the processes of nature, but also the changes that have taken place in the landscape and communities of this place in recent decades. The socio-economic upheaval within the horticultural industry over the last thirty to forty years have undoubtedly made an indelible impact on the way many of these individuals perceive their surrounding environment and the way it is expressed though their spoken narrative.

The concept of 'full circle' has also been explored by local author Natalie Allen, in her book (also named *Full Circle*) which is about the memories of market gardeners and the rise and decline of the industry.[17] In a recorded interview Natalie expresses what the Valley's landscape means to her:

> NA: I still don't know why anyone…why grandfather suddenly thought to himself I've got my old scrubland down here, I'll work hard to dig it all out and plant cherry trees – and now it's all gone the full circle and gone back to trees again. Although it's admittedly planted with fir trees, which is a crop as opposed to the scrubland which was there before.
>
> KM: Yes, the landscape must have changed dramatically?
>
> NA: You've only got to go down over what we call Tremoan Hill which is a big steep hill leading from St Mellion down to Halton Quay, you can look across to the left part way down that hill, and you can look into Birchenhayes and across at Brentswood, and where before if was neat rows of clear ground – cultivated ground and cherry trees over it, now it's just a mass of conifers standing about thirty foot high, and the outlook has completely changed – completely.
>
> […] whatever man does to nature soon overcomes it and takes it back into trees and shrubs and plants again – it does go back into nature, it's not all completely spoilt – the earth is still underneath the concrete and tarmac. You notice that on a site in Plymouth, where some old houses had been demolished, down at Pennycomequick. Last summer all the site was a mass of wild flowers and it was

Natalie Allen in the Tamar Valley (Photograph copyright of Ted Giffords (2003) and courtesy of Tamar Vallley AONB)

> beautiful, it must have been seeds that had been there for many years, been disturbed and they flowered, and it looked so beautiful because nature had taken it back again.[18]

The narrative of full circle echoes throughout this extract: the concept of it being only just and irreversible that nature always takes back any man-made enterprise. This is clear by her recollection of her grandfather clearing the scrubland at Birchenhayes commenting that 'now it's all gone back to trees again'. Natalie was herself brought up at Birchenhayes Farm, which even though she left there over fifty years ago she still regards it as home and remembers her childhood with great fondness. Within her memory there appears to be a tension between sadness at the loss of the 'man-made' beauty of her childhood environment and the comfort of knowing nature is hidden beneath all that man does. Meinig's theory of the opposing 'landscape concepts' of nature and habitant have clear resonance with the narrative of full circle in the Tamar Valley. Interestingly the memories of childhood environment are transposed upon the present day urban environment of Plymouth and shape the way she perceives the tension between man and nature in various landscape backdrops. This begs the question of why Natalie and others from the Tamar Valley *need to believe* in the narrative of full circle. Although Natalie recognises that the working land has been replaced by fir trees, interestingly others do not make this distinction and the narrative of full circle masks the reality that some of the Valley wooded slopes are 'man-made' rather than purely due the forces of Nature. The impact that the global market has had on the market gardening industry has been discussed in the previous section. Perhaps the narrative of full circle helps many individuals to 'make sense' of their personal departure from working on the land and the social transformations that have consequently come with the decline of the market gardening industry, in part due to the force of external socio-economic change.

Before we continue, it should be remembered that written texts can influence the oral tradition. This is arguably even more so in the case of those intended for the local community. It may not be too far-fetched to suggest the writing of *Full Circle* re-emphasised the preconception of the narrative of 'full circle' within Natalie's and other local people's testimonies. This could be taken as an example of text versions of heritage being absorbed within the collective memory of a locality and its landscape, or at least a two-way process of author influencing community and community influencing the author. Perhaps the narrative of full circle has even influenced my own perceptions of the Valley's landscape. This is suggested by my 'schoolboy error' as an oral historian, when making the assumption in my comment to Natalie that 'the landscape must have changed dramatically'. Before expanding on this argument any further it is necessary to consider my own connection to the Tamar Valley. The traditional view was that the oral historian should be an almost omniscient figure with a completely neutral outlook. Revisionists have more recently challenged this view and argued that the role of the researcher is a vital ingredient in the construction of narratives. Alessandro Portelli argues that the relationship and interaction between the oral historian and the speaker is an intrinsic factor in the creation of historical narratives, in the sense that it moulds the responses of both parties and therefore should be duly acknowledged as part of the 'creation' of history.[19] While working in the Tamar Valley as an oral history fieldworker, my own connection to the area has inevitably shaped my perceptions. For example, the importance of family associations in building trust was clear through my own connections with the Studden family (my mother's maiden name), who were largely from the Calstock area. Some were market gardeners and others sailed river barges along the Tamar.[20] Although my immediate maternal family are Plymouthian, I have always felt a sense of affinity with the Cornish part of the valley through the oral tradition passed down in my family. I have become more conscious of this since researching the subject over the past decade. Many people I interviewed knew members of the Studden family and I instantly felt more 'accepted' through merely mentioning my family connection. This may well be my own desire to be welcomed into the Tamar Valley 'community' and a longing to discover more about my own history. My personal relationship with the Valley's landscape and *community* reflects my own full circle to return back to my roots. Likewise, I am ultimately weaving my own experience of cross-river family ties and 'hybrid' Cornish-Devonian identity into my research of 'border identity' in the Tamar Valley.

Whether textual or oral in origin, subjective or objective in perspective, the narrative of full circle for many inhabitants of the Valley seems to help negotiate its socio-economic and environmental transformation. Furthermore, it is also employed by many individuals to narrate their own history within that landscape and to come to terms with the processes of their own lifetime. The seasons of nature almost seem to replicate the seasons of their lives. This is clear from the narration of Terry Rogers; his family's horticultural supplies and transportation business played an intrinsic part in local market gardening commerce:

> It's a strange life when I look back on it, but an enjoyable life – with its ups and downs. But now the Valley has gone back to how it was before I even knew it. The hills back to growing trees, whereas they'd been cleared by the miners in the depression, now it's all back to the trees growing again. And when I drive around the Valley, ah yes, I can remember that area was all strawberries and flowers, now it's all trees. Then I go down to Brentswood, and I can remember a little narrow lane…and I'd drive a converted private vehicle with room on the back for flowers, and we would collect the flowers and drive to the top – and there was a big drop. And we'd come down through – and I can see Bill Rickard, Johnny Sambles, and I can still see all those – down to Halton Quay, the Reap, to Masons, to Tom Gorman's and up through; and that was one of the rounds we did. It was interesting; it was good fun, sometimes hectic, sometimes quiet.[21]

Terry and Vivian Rogers (Photograph copyright of Ted Giffords (2003) and courtesy of Tamar Vallley AONB)

Within this narrative extract, Terry is fusing his own life story with the cyclical pattern of the Valley's landscape. 'Looking back' over his life and then reverting to a landscape that predates his own existence. The interplay in the processes of human life and the *natural* landscape appear to be even replicated in the rhythm of the speech formation of this wonderful piece of narrative. The 'ups and downs' of life and the changing fortunes of the market gardening communities are almost at one with Terry's mnemonic journey 'up and down' the slopes of the Valley. This also demonstrates how landscapes can be constructed of human beings and not just trees and fields. Within Terry's memory all the families and personalities that he knew are intertwined in the landscape – to him they are just as much part of the landscape as the earth itself. On one level, it could be suggested that the narrative of the landscape turning a full circle reflects the integration of his own life story within the process of nature. It is also a eulogy to the market gardens lying dormant under the trees and undergrowth.

Conclusion: A new narrative for the Valley?

We have explored how the concept of nature turning a full circle can mollify the socio-economic and environmental transformations that have occurred within the Tamar Valley. Nonetheless, physical landscapes in the Valley have not entirely reverted back to the past, and the region faces new challenges and opportunities in the promotion of local produce, as well as in other connected areas such as 'eco-tourism'. In recent years traditional fruit and flower varieties, many unique to the Tamar Valley, have been re-introduced into cultivation, which will hopefully continue the region's horticultural heritage, albeit far less wide-scale than once was.[22]

Perhaps oral history also has a part to play in the economic and social 'sustainability' in the Tamar Valley. Indeed, although an important part of oral history is to preserve the memories of the past, what is the use of listening to the past if it is not used to create a better future? The outreach of oral history is, by its very nature, multifaceted. Audio-visual history has the potential to promote local economic growth and cultural renewal at a macro level. For example, oral history can be used as a promotional aid for selling local produce at markets and in shops, revealing the *human story* behind the cultivation of those crops. Interactive websites which incorporate oral and visual material can be used to promote local heritage and tourism at a global scale. As a cautionary note however, there is also a need for an 'educated heritage' that celebrates the distinctiveness of the Valley's heritage, but does not gloss over the social and economic problems that continue in this region.[23] Moreover, the dissemination of oral history in exhibitions, websites and installations is at its most effective when local communities are consulted at various key points and encouraged to be involved in the creation of their own histories, rather than a concept of 'heritage' being transplanted externally.

In this vein, oral history also has the inbuilt ability to explore the complexities of memory and the intricate fabric of human emotions – both so integral to public history. It can explore identity beyond pre-defined categories such as birthplace or ethnicity, which is particularly relevant to border regions such as the Tamar Valley. This is not to deny the fact that the Tamar is a tangible border of great cultural and historical importance. But it also needs to be acknowledged that there is also another level of spatial identity based upon a 'sense of place' that traverses both sides of the river.

Notes

I wish to acknowledge the European Social Fund's support of CAVA's research in the Tamar Valley.

1. Interview of Terry Rogers, AVI/091, CAVA, November 2002.
2. For further information on this debate see: Kayleigh Milden and Garry Tregidga, 'Reflections on Rescorla: a study of micro-peripheral identity', *Cornish History*, Cornish History Network , 2002,
3. Interview of Gerald Veale, AVI/095, CAVA, May 2002.
4. For examples of 'revisionist' approaches to oral history see Alessandro Portelli, The *Death of Luigi Trastulli and Other Stories: Form and Meaning in Oral History*, State University of New York Press, Albany, 1991; Alessandro Portelli, *The Battle of Valle Giulia*, University of Wisconsin Press, Wisconsin, 1997; Luisa Passerini, *Fascism in Popular Memory*, Cambridge University Press, Cambridge, 1987, pp. 1-59, 127-49.
5. *The Evening Herald*, 6 October 2010, p.7.
6. Philip Payton, 'Territory and Identity' in Philip Payton (ed.), *Cornwall Since the War*, Dyllansow Truran, 1993, pp. 224-31.
7. 'Cornwall: County or Country?' (Programme One), South West Film and Television Archive, c.1973.
8. 'Cornwall: County or Country?', South West Film and Television Archive, 1982.
9. Kayleigh Milden, 'A Much Contested Border: The Dynamics of Cultural Memory Regarding the Cornwall-Devon Border', *Celtic Cultural Studies*, 2007: http://www.celtic-cultural-studies.com/papers/02/milden-01.html
10. Interview of John and Iris Snell, AVI/096, CAVA, May 2002.
11. See Maurice Halbwachs, *On Collective Memory* (edited by Lewis A. Coser), The University of Chicago Press, 1992.
12. Denis Cosgrove, *Social Formation and Symbolic Landscape*, Taylor and Francis, 1984, p.66.
13. *Ibid*, p.13.
14. D.W. Meinig, 'The Beholding Eye: ten versions of the same scene' in D.W. Meinig (ed.), *The Interpretation of Ordinary Landscapes*, Oxford, 1979, pp. 34-6.
15. Refer to interviews of George Brown, AVI/090, May 2002; Mary Clarke Eastment, AVI/189, May 2002; Doug Richards, AVI/321, May 2002; Ruth Woolcock, AVI/090, November 2002, all CAVA.
16. Patrick Laviolette, 'Landscaping Death: Resting Places for Cornish Identity', *Journal of Material Culture* 8. 2, London 2003, pp.215-8.
17. Natalie Allen, *Full Circle*, Saltash, 2000.
18. Interview of Natalie Allen, AVI/083, CAVA, November 2002.
19. Alessandro Portelli, *The Battle of Valle Giulia: Oral History and the Art of Dialogue*, Wisconsin, 1997, pp. 3-88.
20. By 'barge people' I mean people who used to transport local produce along the River Tamar by boat.
21. Interview of Terry Rogers, CAVA, AVI/091, November 2002.
22. One example is Mary Martin, who has reintroduced old apple and cherry varieties back into cultivation in Valley. Another is the launch of the book, Sovereigns, *Madams and Double Whites*, organised by the Tamar Valley AONB in May 2004, which promoted local produce at Covent Garden, London. See *Western Morning News*, 22 May 2005.
23. Based on discussions at 'Listening to the Past - Looking to the Future', CAVA Conference (December 2004, Cornwall Centre Redruth), and 'A Future Strategy for Audio Visual History in the Tamar Valley'; a CAVA workshop in association with Tamar Valley AONB Service (June 2005, Cotehele House).

Cribzilla: The construction of the Cornish surfing myth

Geoff Swallow

'Mountainous waves generate modern myths'[1]

Two crowds gather on a Cornish headland above a crashing sea. The first is of well-to-do Edwardian visitors, most of whom are staying at the Headland Hotel. The 'Newquay Riots' of August 1897 provoked by its construction have faded from memory, and apart from the subservient hotel staff, these visitors have not come into contact with any locals who might recall those events.[2] On this early Sunday morning, when most locals in Methodist Newquay are at Chapel, these visitors have promenaded the empty, firm sands of Fistral beach which, following the opening of the Headland and nearby Atlantic hotels, has undergone a makeover by the guidebooks from 'wild and desolate'[3] to 'a favourite bathing place on account of the long stretch of fine sand.'[4] It is the end of August, too rough for them to have braved bathing from Fistral, where they know that 'only strong and practised swimmers should venture out into the surf':[5] instead, they may have luxuriated in the hotel's hot and cold sea-water baths. In contrast to Fistral, which 'exposed to Westerly winds ... is not so safe as Newquay beach,'[6] and only this month the visiting editor of the *Ilford Guardian* has eulogised the 'perfect' bathing which can be 'indulged in from old-fashioned bathing machines' on the town beach, where in contrast to other resorts '[t]here are no tiresome restrictions against mixed bathing',[7] few people, as yet, bathe at Newquay. Our Edwardian crowd know from Waren's guidebook[8] of the 'surpassingly grand' sight of the huge Atlantic rollers breaking on the Headland, churning the sea to foam and throwing its spray over the rocks: now, standing on the Headland in front of the hotel, they are experiencing for themselves the full awe and power of 'gigantic waves thundering at the cliffs'.[9]

Sixty-one years on, a smaller, noticeably younger and entirely male crowd have gathered on the same spot. It is a 'bright but forbidding'[10] day in September: which for these young men (unlike most of their generation, for whom 1966 will be remembered through the 'patriotic myths' created around the exploits of another group of young men earlier this summer)[11] will be remembered as the year of 'The Great September Swell'.[12] Most of them are locals, some barely teenagers, who have been awake half the night listening to the boom of the sea, knowing that on the rising tide this morning, some of the biggest waves Newquay has ever seen will be breaking off Towan Head,[13] on the reef that in the 1960s only a handful of locals know as Cribbar. Among the 'Newquay boys' are a few older men with a bigger physical presence, whom the youngsters among them treat with a respect bordering on deification: experienced big wave riders from California, Australia and Hawaii, but locals by adoption into the town's fledgling surf community, who today 'word had gone round ... were trying to ride Cribbar.'[14] Unlike their Edwardian counterparts, whose gaze was delimited by the blown spray and the churning white water almost at their feet, the collective gaze of this crowd focuses further out, maybe half a mile, to the tiny figures, which gradually, imperceptibly, paddle their surfboards out through the raging white water to where the face of the wave walls up as high as twenty feet before breaking into 'the biggest clean surf many people [have] ever seen.'[15] The crowd 'feel the ground shake as these monsters ma[k]e landfall'[16]

Two crowds gathering on Newquay's Towan Head, separated by sixty one years, both witnessing the phenomenon known today as The Cribbar. Both my reconstructed accounts are based on published evidence. The first on a report in the local press published a few days after the event in August 1905, the second, on the account of the day in September 1966 when Cribbar was surfed for the first time. It was published in the first history of British surfing and based on interviews by the late Rod Holmes with some of those present on the day. Both these published accounts are, in their way, highly constructed and mediated. Only a few days separates the event of late August 1905 from the description which appeared in the *Newquay Express*. The newspaper's correspondent, who wrote of 'the entire coast line ... edged with the white of seething foam, and the air thick with flying spume and spray', may have been among the crowd on that day, but it is equally likely that he was not. His account owes much to descriptions found in early guidebooks to Newquay published between the 1880s and 1890s.[17] Written for the late season visitors among its readership, this account needs to be seen in the context of the expectations created among visitors by such guidebooks of the 'effects' which were to be experienced from the Headland. By contrast, the 1960s account is constructed through thirty-year-old memories, of eyewitnesses present on the day, many of whom were teenagers, filtered through the experience and hindsight of the middle aged men they had become in the early 1990s. These memories encapsulate not just the perspective of individual, personal life histories but offer a retrospective on the history of British surfing, particularly significantly, as one of the then teenage eye witnesses, Roger Mansfield, is now one of its leading historians.[18]

In the days before the tourism and hotel boom of the 1890s, when the economy of Newquay was centred on its inshore fishing industry and coastal trade, the sheltered harbour which gave it its modern name was the spatial and perceptual focus of the town. Psychologically, as well as physically, Towan Head marked the western extremity of the town's perceptual map. One guidebook description of west-facing Fistral Beach depicted the other side of the headland as an 'unbroken waste of sand, dreary enough as compared to Newquay,'[19] and shows that it was then still regarded as separate from the town. Like the early maps of medieval navigators, Towan Head marked the limit of the 'known' world, beyond which Fistral represented a *terra incognita*, 'wild' and 'desolate' well into the 1890s.[20] For generations of Newquay fishermen, boats leaving the safety of the harbour and heading west had almost immediately to negotiate not just the Headland itself, against the prevailing westerly winds, but, also depending on the state of the tide and swell, the reef that extends a mile or so under the sea from it.

On Ordnance Survey maps, this reef is marked as 'Cribbar Rocks.' In Cornish *krib* means comb, crest, reef (of rocks); *kriba* is a verb, meaning (to) split into fragments; *kribas* a verb, meaning to comb.[21] It was common for Cornish placenames to be anglicised by early map makers. Headlands, as landmarks for shipping navigating the heavily indented Cornish coast were particularly susceptible to anglicisation, one example being *Innyall*, from the Cornish 'desolate place', which was renamed Gurnard's Head by mid-eighteenth century English mapmakers from its imagined resemblance to the fish's profile. In the case of Cribbar, whilst it retained a Cornish component, the cartographers' lack of understanding of the literal meaning of its Cornish name, led to the tautological 'Cribbar Rocks.' The name Cribbar also contains a secondary denotation of the conspicuous 'comb' of white water[22] marking its location at the most dangerous state of the tide, which as late as the 1940s fishermen would still detour a quarter of a mile to avoid.[23]

It is not unusual for Cornish words to have survived in modified form in dialect, local placenames or technical terms specific to traditional industries. A number of these survivors are documented in Morton Nance's *Glossary of Cornish Sea-Words*.[24] Yet Cribbar does not appear in Morton Nance's study, either as the generic term for reef, or specifically in relation to the reef off Towan Head. 'Cribbar' is one of only a handful of Cornish words to have been perpetuated in the vocabulary of 'surf-bathing' (as it was known in the inter-war years) and surfing in Cornwall. All of those, significantly, are used to denote a place of danger, threat and fear. Other examples being the *vellas* of Perranporth implicated in drowning accidents in the 1930s[25] and the *Gowna* rocks which, in the early days of the surf lifesaving movement in St Ives in the late 1950s, were synonymous with the dangers of rip currents off Porthmeor beach.[26] Given that sea bathing was part of a process of outsider colonisation of the Cornish coast, and one originally practised by visitors of a generally higher social and economic status than the indigenous Cornish, we can surmise that these linguistic appropriations were part of the perpetuation of a stereotype of the Cornish as foreign, primitive and barbaric, linked to early representations of their coast as an inhospitable, dangerous and fearful place.[27] Unlike Cribbar, metamorphosing in recent years into The Cribbar, and shifting its meaning in the process from the reef to the wave, neither of these other terms survived the domestication of the Cornish coast brought about by the tourism boom of the 1960s onwards.

For the locals who first encountered Cribbar it was a site of danger to be negotiated against the prevailing winds, between the shelter of the harbour and the exposed open sea of the fishing grounds. It was both a physical and psychological barrier not just between safety and danger, livelihood and poverty, but symbolically between the

known and the unknown, between life and death itself. The detailed local knowledge that enabled fishermen to read the tides, ground and wind swell and the currents created by Cribbar, and avoid its dangers, would have been passed as an oral tradition through generations of fishing families. This created a close and highly specialised occupational 'place-memory' which, as John Conway's contribution to Holmes and Wilson's account suggests, may have survived into the inter-war years of the industry's decline.[28]

But from at least the middle of the nineteenth century, the complex local place-knowledge Cribbar represented was already fading. This is evidenced from extensive research in local newspaper accounts of shipwrecks in the area.[29] Although many of them refer to Towan Head and The Island (the knuckled end of the Headland where our two crowds gathered), none refer to Cribbar by name. When the steamer Syracuse was wrecked in a storm in March 1897 for example, one local weekly newspaper described how 'about six feet of the masts of [the] vessel are now visible above the water… about two miles northward of the Headland' without naming the reef on which it had run aground.[30] This suggests that by 1897, the complex place-knowledge of Cribbar, which had formed part of the lived, collective memory of the town for generations had already been lost in the demographic and social change that came with the rapid expansion and modernisation of its economic transition from fishing to tourism.

Beach crowd with Newquay lifeboat in the early 1900s (Postcard from Mac Waters Collection)

Changing guidebook representations show a process through which, as part of this expansion between the 1880s and 1900s, Newquay colonised, incorporated and domesticated the *terra incognita* to the west. From being the physical and psychological boundary that separated Newquay from the 'unmitigated violence of the ocean',[31] beyond which lay only the 'wild and desolate' Fistral beach, Towan Head itself became the vantage point from which visitors could gaze upon the awe and spectacle of the sea breaking 'on the submerged rocks which form [the Headland's] westernmost point'.[32] Crucial to this development, which literally changed the visitor's perspective on Newquay, were the development of the Atlantic Hotel (1892) and Headland Hotel (1900), constructed on Towan Head itself, by Cornish architect and entrepreneur Silvanus Trevail. Perry has described the 'unashamedly elitist dream' Trevail brought to the siting and design of these hotels, as landmark buildings originally intended as part of an unrealised master plan of broad esplanades, mansions set in their own grounds and terraced boulevards of villas. They were all conceived on the same scale and luxury as the Grand Hotels he had visited in continental spas and resorts like Biarritz.[33] The Headland Hotel in its exposed setting can be seen as representing the binaries of 'civilisation' and 'primitivism'.[34] Sticking out into the Atlantic, this 'monumental' building literally and symbolically provided a new perspective from which visitors could experience the ruggedness, remoteness, isolation and west-facing exposure to the Atlantic which epitomised Romantic Cornwall.

The hotel, with its hot and cold seawater baths at the turn of a tap, symbolised the triumph of Edwardian technological control over the elements, and the appropriation of the headland as an extension of the socially constructed boundaries of the hotel, was part of the same discourse. When the visitor to the hotel left its confines, he exposed himself to elemental dangers, but did so in the belief that the safety and comforts of the hotel, with its modern devices, extended its protection against them. The Edwardian guest was invited to regard the Headland itself as an extension of the hotel grounds. In this context, the description of the 'crowds of visitors flock[ing] to the Headland…to see the huge Atlantic rollers tumbling in on the Fistral Beach,'[35] can be seen as part of the tourism construction of Edwardian Newquay as an upmarket health resort, into which Cribbar is co-opted as a site/sight for the emergent 'tourist gaze'.

This is the transitional point at which the dominant nineteenth century romantic discourse of the sea yields to the rational, scientific, medical discourse which influenced much seaside resort development in the early twentieth century. The headland is represented at once as a site of potential danger ('the air thick with flying spume and spray'), and as a site with health-giving properties.[36] The crowd standing on the headland is described as if partaking of a medical cure: '[t]he air was very decidedly salt, and the amount of ozone prevailing must have been considerable.'[37] Most significantly, the surf zone is denoted as a liminal space[38] neither land or sea, where '[g]igantic waves thunder … with a fury quite awe-inspiring, sending up clouds of flying spray just, for all the world, like smoke from some big explosion,' a battlefield where cultures and ideologies clash and territories are contested, offering the equal possibility of re-invigoration (life) or oblivion (death).

The imagination of medieval man populated the spaces between the boundaries of the known world and the *terra incognita* that lay beyond, with monsters. I suggest that the residual place memory of the local fishing community, and the liminal site/sight

constructed through the tourist gaze for the Edwardian visitor at the newly colonised edge of Newquay's 'known world', the 'patriotic myths' of 1966 and the creation of a foundation myth of British surfing, all combined to give birth to the modern legend of The Cribbar. By the 1960s it appears that Cribbar as a place memory only survived through oral accounts embodied in stories told by Newquay's dwindling number of fishermen. A good example was the late John Conway.[39] He recalls as a boy fishing by the Fly Cellars and seeing 'the remains of large yachts … pounded to matchwood off Cribbar', but despite three people allegedly having been drowned in this incident, I have not been able to find any reports in local newspapers of this event. It is difficult to substantiate the extent to which Cribbar was still a living part of the collective place-memory of Newquay, or whether this was personal to Conway, from family or other connections with the Newquay fishing community. Even in the surfing press, references to Cribbar are almost non-existent before the publication of Holmes and Wilson's book in 1994. A letter in the surf magazine *Wavelength* in 1992 refers to an interview about the Cribbar with one of the early Newquay surfers to which the editor replies 'the Cribbar was ridden last winter … but we don't have any photos in back issues. Ask Newquay legend Roy Langton how heavy it was, he snapped his [board] that day … Definitely not a wave for the faint-hearted.'[40]

Whilst it is perhaps risky to draw any firm conclusions from such limited documentary evidence, it seems that Cribbar's significance as a site of fear and danger diminished as the fishing industry declined. With Newquay's economic focus shifting from

Newquay Harbour in the early 1900s (Postcard from Mac Waters Collection)

fishing to tourism, the town's topographical focus shifted also. This literally provided a different perspective on Cribbar, as a site/sight of spectacle which could be experienced from a vantage point of safety. The older, residual place memory of Cribbar appears to have been perpetuated into the 1990s only through the stories of local surfers, and seems to have been transmitted orally. Although this has to be a provisional conclusion for now, it seems to have been the older, 'first generation' of Newquay surfers, from the 1960s, who preserved and passed on that knowledge, at least until the publication of Holmes and Wilson's book in 1994, when it entered the imagination of a wider public.

Most surf historians are, or have been, themselves surfers. The tanned, blonde surfing pioneers of the 1960s and 70s have metamorphosed into the grizzled chroniclers of their own lives and times. Inevitably, the type of histories they construct tends to the andecdotal and mythologizing, inevitably foregrounding their own involvement, that of their peers and that of their own locality. Surfing shares many of the elements and motifs of epic narrative – the quest, or search for the perfect wave, the struggle with a powerful, elemental adversary, conquest (or failure) – which are consciously or unconsciously reinforced in the retelling. Surfing is a rich oral culture[41] with its origins in the non-literate, oral tradition of pre-contact Hawaiian culture which was remembered and transmitted between generations in myths, stories, songs and chants. The modern Hawaiian social practice known as 'talking story', is a direct continuation of this tradition.[42]

The dominant form of surf historiography, as represented by Holmes and Wilson, has been reconstructionist. They use a traditional narrative structure, and focus on specific events which are reported 'objectively' (except for the presence of the first person narrator). Points are presented as 'facts' through a process of simple historical recovery, mainly based on their own reminiscences or those of their contemporaries. Through repeated retelling to a receptive audience (who in many cases are often themselves co-participants in the story), over time these anecdotes have accreted into ritualised narratives which have become more real than the reality itself. Inevitably they contrast the present with a nostalgic yearning for the past, for the golden age of their youth when waves were bigger and line ups were less crowded. These personalised accounts tend to reify certain 'stand outs', pivotal figures, waves and events with iconic, even legendary status.

As the title of a surfing history, *You Should Have Been Here Yesterday* is uncompromisingly clear on where it stands. Although at one level it can be read as uncomplicatedly nostalgic, it implicitly divides those who 'were here' from those who were not, conferring on them a status and entitlement to claim 'ownership' as originators and guardians of that history. Deconstructing '[t]he crafted yet powerful coherence of narratives in terms of their powerful implications … in the construction of a personal past through the process of memory,' therefore raises issues of objectivity and sensitivity for the cultural historian who may not having been 'here yesterday'. Noting 'the provisional, contested and contextual nature of the surfing narrative' in their sociological study of surfing, Ford and Brown suggest the need for a more rigorous application of the 'conceptual tools of narrative history … to delineate the ways in which the selectivity and unfolding of cultural authority of such histories reflect the pattern and structures

inherent in the human cultural process of storymaking.'[43]

Many of the structural components of myth described by Levi-Strauss are to be found in Holmes and Wilson's account. Its narrative structure is what Levi-Strauss terms 'slated', that is, built up of layers through which, although discontinuous and intercutting between four different narrative voices, the story itself runs continuously. Each of the interwoven testimonies has a clear role within the overall construction of the story. Holmes himself, whose interviews with eye witnesses form the basis of the account, provides the overall narrative framework for the story, his opening paragraph introducing most of the thematic elements (what Levi Strauss calls the 'mythemes') of what has since become the 'Cribbar myth':

> Older surfers tell tales of when swells seemed bigger, lasted longer and had a classic, never to be repeated quality. We all do it, sooner or later. No matter where you live, every surf beach has its day, a time when the variables of wind, tide and swell combine to offer an all-time session. It's a day when the usual wave indicators make no sense; when giant sets shake the cliff top; when take off and paddle out points are nothing like the regular set up; when the horizon lifts like the end of the world; when only a handful are ready and willing to meet the challenge.[44]

In his contribution to the account, Conway looks back from 1966 to the Cribbar of the 1940s as an age of innocence: "Thirty years ago, Cribbar always looked to be breaking better because maybe we didn't know a lot about big waves. Perhaps it looked to be a better wave than it does today because people had limited experience."[45] Looking back from the then-present (i.e. 1994) to Cribbar in the 1960s, he laments '[t]he peaks seem to have changed out there. I don't recall seeing it work exactly how it used to. The reef

Postcard sent from Headland Hotel in 1907 (Postcard from Mac Waters Collection)

went through a period in the mid-sixties of really coming on, throwing up mountainous conditions. But there doesn't seem to be much interest in riding it now.'[46] By contrast, also looking back from 1994 Chris Jones offers a counter-view: 'But I saw Cribbar working perfectly, five or six years ago, breaking right round the Point and into Little Fistral, so as far as I know, the good days weren't confined to the sixties. Some days have been ten or fifteen feet and just perfect in the winter-time.'[47] Although these two voices appear to contradict each other, they are better seen as a binary pairing, with a single role in the construction of one of the key themes of the Cribbar myth, which is its fickleness and unpredictability.

Roger Mansfield's description of the 'epic performance' of the men who attempted to surf Cribbar that day in 1966, sits at the heart of Holmes and Wilson's multi-layered account. It contributes the epic motifs of struggle and adversity, which contain the possibility of failure as well as success that have since become a key motif of the Cribbar myth. Two of the three attempts that he describes actually end in failure, one of which significantly allows him as adult narrator to give his teenage counterpart a 'walk on' part in his own narrative, when he rescues the two halves of one of the surfers' shattered boards from a gully in the rocks. Failure elevates the surfers in Mansfield's account to flawed, but heroic figures. Although mediated through a thirty-year-old memory, Mansfield's graphic description of watching the first surfer to ride Cribbar has the immediacy of something happening before our own eyes:

> [Pete Russell] was half way down the wave before I realised that this giant was being ridden. I heard others shouting 'Wait … look … it is!' and there was a white scar snaking down the left wave face, with a bigger twist in it as Pete turned on the wave down. It was so far out, it was so big, the whitewater was rolling slowly. It seemed everything was in slow motion.'[48]

For us, reading this description, it is not just that everything is slowed down, but that time is brought to a standstill. What Mansfield holds up to us in the description quoted above is not so much a memory, as a 'photographic' simulacrum of a memory. Although the memory is personal to Mansfield, and clearly triggered for him by the Proustian recall of that shout, what I hear resounding through the years is the sound of a camera lens capturing not a specific moment on a specific wave, but the archetypal image of the big wave.

One important narrative perspective that I have left out of this structural analysis so far is that of Doug Wilson. As Alan Trachtenberg has noted, '[i]mages become history more than traces of specific events in the past, when they are used to interpret the present in the light of the past, when they are presented and received as explanatory accounts of collective reality. They become history when they are conceived "as symbolic events in a shared culture".'[49] I suggest that the 'collective reality' represented by Wilson's images is crucial to the myth of The Cribbar. The 'bright but forbidding',[50] 'bright but misty day'[51] with its unnatural blueness, mediated through the unnatural colours of 1960s Ektachrome is an important contributor to the retrospective idealisation of the wave that day as 'insane walls of deep blue power'.[52] Writing the captions to these photographs thirty years later, this may have been what Holmes had in mind

Early surf bathing at Newquay (Postcard from Mac Waters Collection)

when he made comparisons between these and images of big surf in Hawaii: one photo caption describes a 'right hand barrel destroy[ing] itself on Towan Head' as '[l]ooking more like the North Shore than the North Coast',[53] another of Cribbar as 'looking more like Sunset Beach'.[54]

Yet I suggest that there is another theme at work here, which can be found in an article written by Mansfield also in 1994, which links the myth of the Cribbar to the 'myth of ancestry' that trace the descent of different surf cultures directly from the ancient rituals, hierarchies and taboos of pre-contact Polynesian surf culture through its ethnic Hawaiian 'founding fathers' of the modern era.[55] In that article, Mansfield puts forward what I would call the 'two oceans' thesis, within which, in explicitly postcolonial terms, he reverses the power relations between the colonised 'tropical island beach dwellers' of the Pacific and the colonising 'white Englishmen wishing to go surfing in cold northern seas' of the Atlantic. My 'two oceans thesis' refers to the way that during the 1960s we begin to see a deliberate elision of Cornwall's 'Atlantic rollers' with the surf waves of the Pacific: invoking Hawaii, as in the example of Cornwall's North Coast with Hawaii's North Shore, but also Australia (Bondi) and California (Malibu), which were increasingly used as archetypes of idealised surfing locations in guidebook representations of Cornish beaches.[56] We see this perpetuated in more recent accounts in the popular press, in which the Cribbar is transformed into the archetype of the big wave, conferring on Cornwall shared space alongside Hawaii in the media's construction of surfing.[57]

Significantly in this context, it was Hawaiian and Australian surfers who first rode Cribbar on the day described in Holmes and Wilson: 'Jack [Lydgate] … a big wave rider from Hawaii who knew about massive surf … Aussie Johnny McIlroy, and Sydney surfer Pete Russell'.[58] As a surf historian, Mansfield has developed a very strong anthropological sense of surfers as a 'tribe', and this informs both his Cribbar testimony and his own writings on the origins of British surfing.[59] In his 1994 article for instance, he describes early images of 'Hawaiians gliding shoreward standing on boards, *as of Gods*, propelled by the waves (my italics),'[60] and represents the arrival of surfing in Britain as a 'gift' from the ancient gods, conferred through the agency of their direct descendants, the modern day surfing Hawaiians. If Mansfield's 'The Source' is British surfing's myth of origin, Holmes and Wilson's account of the Cribbar is its myth of coming of age: that Cribbar was ridden for the first time by Hawaiian (and Australian) surfers is hugely symbolic, conferring the approval of the gods on British surfing, and elevating Cribbar to the status of a world-class wave. In that summer of 'patriotic myths', the Great September Swell of 1966 provided British surfing with one of its own most powerful founding myths.

Among the 'mythemes' of the Cribbar account, we can identify the shape-shifting, transformative and metamorphosing qualities through which the familiar is changed into something unfamiliar: 'when the usual wave indicators make no sense; when giant sets shake the cliff top; when take off and paddle out points are nothing like the regular set up; when the horizon lifts like the end of the world'.[61] Chris Jones' description confers life and agency on the inanimate Mystic Rock, which he found 'just monstrous. It got it's name (sic) because sometimes it's there and sometimes it isn't, it's mysterious. I paddled into one and down in the trough, I could actually see the old Mystic in shallow water in front of me. There it was, that big old solid lump, which few have ever seen, staring back at me.'[62] This last description contains another important element of the Cribbar myth: anthropomorphised, rarely seen, it is unpredictable, threatening and malevolent.

The vocabulary which surfers use to describe waves lends itself to anthropomorphism: shoulder, face, lip. In Holmes and Wilson, the waves are described as 'giants',[63] and 'monsters'.[64] Russell is quoted as describing the experience as 'surreal'[65] and there are elements of surrealism in which the face of the wave metamorphoses from a glassy 'cliff face' to the face of a living creature: 'paddling hard and deep, each clawed his way into the shallow faced 15 foot lumps, before taking a drop that came direct from their own nightmares.' The 'face' of the moving water takes on the properties of flesh, at which the surfers claw: 'their hand holes of white water pocking the surface and just clipping the pitching lip which must have been two or three feet thick ...' As in a nightmare, it grows bigger as they struggle to climb it: 'when Jack Lydgate paddled up one wave he left three hand-hole paddle marks in the face – and he wasn't even at the top. He was riding an eleven foot board.'[66] Mansfield employs a similar metaphor, describing the only one of the three surfers to ride 'this giant' as leaving 'a white scar snaking down the left wave face.'[67] Given the lack of references to Cribbar in the popular print and broadcast media before the publication of Holmes and Wilson's account, compared to the explosion of media interest in it after 1994, this was undoubtedly its route into the wider public imagination. Although created by the media, visitors and surfers themselves have since helped to engender a place mythology around 'The Cribbar', showing how '[p]lace mythologies are enacted through practices, however, rather than image alone.'[68]

The clue to the myth lies in the intrusion of that definite article, and the way that as 'The Cribbar' it has tapped into earlier constructions of the Cornish coast, and of a *terra incognita* that has persisted and survived the layering of more modern constructions: 'here there be monsters.' Media representations have built on Holmes and Wilson and the elements of the unpredictability and infrequency of its return to represent the Cribbar anthropomorphically for the popular imagination. Most crucially, the depiction of the wave as 'a monster' or 'a giant' to be sought out and pursued, has transformed it into the pursuer, no longer safely 'out there' but a threat which rises unpredictably out of the sea to devour not just the surfer who trespasses onto its territory, but any one of us.

In 2006, Mansfield published his own version of his Cribbar account on his website. It is, as one would expect, similar to that constructed by Holmes and Wilson, but there are some significant differences that serve to distance his own first-person account from theirs. Although he describes one of Wilson's photographs as 'look[ing] eerily like Sunset Beach, Hawaii,' he is conscious that what he is describing is a photographic representation and not what, on the day, he recalls seeing, opening up a gap between the event and its re-construction as myth. In contrast to the idealisation and exoticisation of the wave described in Holmes and Wilson's account, Mansfield recalls the 'raw sewage [that] was gushing out around the headland. [The surfers] all looked back in disgust as if to say 'What are we doing?' but their attention was totally focused on the long paddle and the huge heavy swell.'[69] In the 1960s, untreated sewage was a hazard all around the Cornish coast, but whilst visually unpleasant to visitors, there were then few surfers to be directly affected by it. By 1990, the number of surfers had increased exponentially, and the influential environmental pressure group Surfers Against Sewage (SAS) was set up to campaign against it. During the early 1990s, the problems of sewage and other toxic wastes in the sea had become one of the most contested issues in surfing, as evidenced by the surfing press of the period. In 1991 *Wavelength* reported Fistral beach had been declared unsafe by South West Water, whose Managing Director was quoted as saying: 'If you want to stay healthy don't go surfing at Newquay.'[70] Next to the letter about Cribbar published in *Wavelength* in 1992, was a letter headed 'Toxic Mutant Sewage Surfers'.[71] This relates to the 1990s cartoon series Teenage Mutant Ninja Turtles, suggesting an interesting connection between surfing and urban myths of the day which reflected fears about the effects of toxicity in sewage waste. The TMNT lived in the sewers, the mutated product of toxic waste. Just as the fictional film monster Godzilla was first created by the Japanese in 1954 as an allegory of nuclear weapons,[72] I suggest that we can read into the Cribbar myth similar allegoric meanings relating to surfers' fear of the effects of raw sewage being discharged into the sea off Towan Head. This is not explicit in Holmes and Wilson's account, which in its conflation of Towan Head and Sunset Beach idealises and exoticises a reality which, as Mansfield's website account suggests, was far from accurate in 1966, and was giving rise to increasing concern by the time their mythologizing account was published in 1994.

In the 1960s, because of its inconsistency and size, the Cribbar was regarded as a potentially rideable wave by only a handful of surfers, those who, according to Holmes and Wilson, 'really knew what they were about.' Critically, these were surfers who had

experience of big wave conditions elsewhere, like Jack Lydgate, 'a big wave rider from Hawaii who knew about massive surf.'[73] As images of big waves in places like Hawaii became more accessible to British surfers from the 1970s onwards, through surfing magazines, and increasingly films, those who lacked such first-hand experience were perhaps able to get Cribbar into better perspective. To those more familiar with images of twenty or thirty feet or higher waves, which in the famous words of Hawaiian big surf pioneer Buzzy Trent 'are not measured in feet, but in increments of fear',[74] a 'mere' ten or fifteen feet, however perfect, is not the stuff of legend.

By the late 1990s when 'The Cribbar' moved into the popular imagination through the national press, its elusiveness had become one of the central elements of the myth, and the challenge of predicting when it would break had become as challenging as riding the wave itself. In December 2004, the *London Evening Standard* described it as 'a rare swell called The Cribbar, [which] occurs only once or twice a year and lasts no more than an hour or two.'[75] In December 2005, the BBC reported on it as 'the legendary and rarely seen wave off North Cornwall'. In February 2006, the *Independent* reported it as 'famously inconsistent, appearing about once or twice a year',[76] and in January 2008 the *Daily Mail* as 'the legendary wave which only happens once a year.'[77] The Cribbar completed its metamorphosis from reef to wave, mutating on the way into a sea monster, in press reports from about 2002. These built on the elements of unpredictability and infrequency of its return. Rep-resentations of the wave as something for heroic surfers to pursue also shifted, to the wave as the pursuer. In January 2006 *Western Morning News* billboards announced 'Newquay's Giant Cribbar Wave Returns.'[78] Rafferty's observations on Godzilla seem especially relevant in this context: in such 'pop creations … the blunt metaphors, like the monsters themselves, tend to develop minds of their own: they run rampant, flattening even the sturdiest intentions.'[79] Although mostly found in the mainstream press, this anthropomorphic representation has also, surprisingly, been taken up by the specialist surfing press. In February 2006 the website Surfers Village Global Surf News carried the headline 'Conquering the Cribbar sea monster.'[80] It was based on an account headed 'I conquered a real sea monster' which had been published in the South Wales newspaper, *Western Mail*,[81] whilst the *Sun* took the sea monster image a stage further, captioning a photograph as '[t]his monster swell, called the Cribbar wave, reached 30ft high as it thundered towards the Cornish coast.'

The Cribbar near the Headland Hotel (Photograph by Tony Plant)

Most recently, representations of The Cribbar entered a new stage in its mutation, when in January 2008 the *Daily Mail* reported it as 'a 30ft monster known as the Cribbar or the 'widow maker'.[82] It is unclear how it acquired this name – certainly no one has yet died whilst trying to surf The Cribbar – but in July 2008 the *Daily Telegraph* had a similar article in relation to Newquay.[83] The dangers of taking on The Cribbar are explicit in all of these representations of it as a monster. Those who do so are described, or in the case of Simon Jayham's account in the *Western Mail*, describe themselves, in terms similar to those of epic tales as heroic figures venturing out to seek the monster in its lair. Thus, '[t]he Cribbar is a near-mythical wave among surfers, found over a mile off the coast of Cornwall'. In Jayham's somewhat self-glorifying account, preparation to meet with the Cribbar incorporates elements of stalking a dangerous quarry, a military campaign and of the ritual preparation of a victim for propitiatory sacrifice.

Ironically, at the same time that popular media interest in The Cribbar has increased, many of the mythic elements of its representation have been undermined by technological advances such as weather satellites and mid-Atlantic wave bouys which provide easily accessible and accurate data for surf forecasting websites.[84] This includes improved telecommunications such as webcams and mobile phones which enable surfers to get up-to-the-minute information on the state of the surf, and the development of 'tow-in' surfing, 'widely regarded as 'the most significant break-through in big wave surfing history'.[85] Advances in digital photography and printing technology have contributed to the 'insider' familiarity of surfers with images of big waves through the surf media, but also the democratisation of the moving image, and video sharing websites like YouTube has made them available to a wider, non-surfing 'outsider' audience.[86] Since the 1960s, when images of big Pacific waves were rare, and most surfers' perceptions of waves was geographically and imaginatively limited by their own local break,[87] through films,[88] DVDs, websites, and magazines, British surfers are now regularly exposed to the biggest waves in the world, among which The Cribbar barely ranks.

Notes

1. Ben Finney and James Houston, *Surfing, the Sport of Hawaiian Kings*, 1966, p.89, quoted in Tanis Thorne, 'Legends of the Surfer Subculture: Part One', *Western Folklore*, Vol 35, No. 3 (July 1976), pp.209-217
2. For the Newquay Riots of August 1895 see Ronald Perry and Hazel Harradence *Silvanus Trevail: Cornish Architect and Entrepreneur*, London, 2008, 141-142
3. J. C. Oliver, *Olivers Illustrated Guide to Newquay and Neighbourhood*, pub M. Marks, The Library, Fore Street, Newquay 1884, p. 12
4. W. H. K. Wright, *Hartnoll's Illustrated Handbook to Newquay and North Cornwall*, pub Hartnoll Brothers, Printers, Publishers and Stationers, Guardian Office, Newquay (new and revised edition, undated but between 1892 and 1897), 12
5. Fanny Goddard and Beatrix F. Cresswell, *The Homeland Handbooks*, Vol 27, Newquay, (2nd edition, 1906), 22. As a measure of how guidebooks tried to accommodate the contradictions between the dangers of bathing and its co-option into the discourse of health, by the 1922 edition this warning had been modified to 'only strong swimmers should venture out into the surf.' (22nd edition, 1922, pp.15-16)
6. *Hartnoll's*, p.12
7. 'A Holiday in the West (by the editor of the Ilford Guardian)', *Newquay Express*, 18 August 1905
8. R. H. Curtis, *Waren's Guide to Newquay and Neighbourhood,* pub F. Waren Photographer and Stationer, Newquay 1899 (4th edition) p.17
9. *Newquay Express*, 25 August 1905
10. Homes and Wilson, 1994, 84, p.87
11. For a critical perspective on the 'patriotic myths subsequently associated with [England's World Cup victory of 1966], see Dominic Sandbrook, *White Heat: A History of Britain in the Swinging Sixties* 2006, 291-306. 'England's victory in the World Cup felt less like the dawn of a new era and more like the last day of a long, lazy summer about to be swept away

in the winds of autumn' (306).

12. http://www.rogermansfield.com/cribbar.html accessed 19.02.08
13. Holmes and Wilson 1994, p.84
14. Holmes and Wilson, 1994, p.87
15. Holmes and Wilson, 1994, p.84
16. Holmes and Wilson, 1994, photo caption, p.87
17. For example, *Olivers* (1884) describes 'frothing foam being carried completely over the Headland,' p.26; *Hartnoll's* (1890s) 'foamy crests, sending high over the Headland large balls of foam', 26; and *Waren's* (4th edition, 1899) 'foam, which is caught by the wind and carried high into the air, like giant snow flakes', p.17. Interestingly, the motif of the foam ball reappears in Holmes and Wilson, , 'disembowel[ling] itself on the reef,' and represented in modern terms as being 'the size of an average semi.' 1994, p.85.
18. Roger Mansfield: 'Rod Holmes (deceased) interviewed me at my home for the material in his book. No-nothing previously written down/prepared. In deed (sic) one mans spontaneous recall (and all the prejudicial inaccuracies that process can produce). However, I always felt a well developed 'sense of place' for what I said.' e-mail to Geoff Swallow, 9 September 2008
19. *Olivers*, 1884, p.12
20. *Waren's*, 1899, p.14
21. Ken George, *Gerlyver Kernewek Kemmyn, (Dictionary of Common Cornish)*, Cornish Language Board 2000, p.79
22. "The special attraction of the Headland … is the fine display afforded by the huge Atlantic rollers as they dash themselves on the ridge of partially or wholly submerged rocks which forms its westernmost point, or gathering into a huge billow or 'comber', curl over and crash down in a swirl of foam upon an outlying rock." Waren's, 1899, 17
23. Holmes and Wilson, 1994, p.82
24. Robert Morton Nance, *A Glossary of Cornish Sea Words*, Federation of Old Cornwall Societies 1963.
25. "Vellas" on Cornish Coast', *The Times*, 10 August 1931, pg 12, col C. Morton Nance (1963) gives the definition 'a pit in sand below water' derived from Cornish fell le, 'a dangerous place'.
26. Robert Morton Nance, 'Why Gowna?' *Old Cornwall*, 5 (1954) pp.164-169; see also Gowna & Cowloe Rocks Cornish – L Archives website http:archiver.rootsweb.com/th/read/CORNISH/2003-05/1052315616 accessed 19.02.2008
27. Geoff Swallow, 'A Foot In The Surf Or A Body In The Waves': surfing's early formation in the cultural construction of place in Cornwall 1906-1966 unpublished MA dissertation, Institute of Cornish Studies, University of Exeter, 2008
28. John Conway quoted in Holmes and Wilson, 1994, 82-83
29. For a useful summary of the principal wrecks at this location between 1854 and 1912, see Clive Carter, *Cornish Shipwrecks* Vol 2: The North Cornish Coast 1970, 121-123
30. *Newquay Visitors Notes and Directory* Vol 2 no 34, 3 March 1897
31. *Oliver's* 1884, p.12
32. *Waren's* (sic) 1889, p.17
33. Perry, (1999),p. 38
34. Ironically, in March 1913 the Lowestoft sailing trawler Renown was wrecked on Towan Head when it mistook the lights of the Headland Hotel for the lighthouse at Trevose Head.
35. *Newquay Express*, 25 August 1905
36, *Newquay Express*, 7 June 1907.
37. *Newquay Express*, Friday 25 August 1905 p.8
38. Fiske, J. (1983) 'Surfalism and Sandiotics: The Beach in Oz Culture'. *Australian Journal of Cultural Studies* http://wwwtds.murdoch.edu.au/-continuum/serial/AJCS/1.2/Fiske.html Vol.1, No.2: pp.120-148.
39. John Conway quoted in Holmes and Wilson 1994, 82-83. Editor of *Wavelength* magazine, Conway was an influential figure in the representation of British surfing culture.
40. *Wavelength*, 37, March/April 1992, p.13
41. 'Surfing legends, tall tales, wonder tales, and fabulates are the genres conspicuous to the folklorist in terms of repetition of themes and characterisations; for fantasy and heroism are the leitmotifs of surf-lore. In many of its manifestations, surf-lore is a special interpretation of historical events and personages; it thus provides the folklorist the opportunity to observe the process of legend formation from fabulate to memorate.' Tanis Thorne, 'Legends of the Surfer Subculture: Part One', *Western Folklore*, Vol 35, No. 3 (July 1976), pp.209-217, 209
42. For the Hawaiian cultural tradition of 'talking story' see for example Stuart Holmes Coleman, *Eddie Would Go: The Story of Eddie Aikau, Hawaiian Hero and Pioneer of Big Wave Surfing*, Yellow Jersey Press, London, 2004, p.52
43. Nick Ford and David Brown, *Surfing and Social Theory: experience, embodiment and narrative of the dream glide*, London, 2006, 170
44. Holmes and Wilson, 1994, p.82
45. John Conway quoted in Holmes and Wilson, 1994, p.82.
46. John Conway quoted in Holmes and Wilson, 1994, p.83. This final comment by the then editor of *Wavelength* is confirmed by the apparent lack of interest shown by the surfing press of the period (see footnote 45)
47. Chris Jones quoted in Holmes and Wilson, 1994, p.83
48. Roger Mansfield quoted in Holmes and Wilson, 1994, p.89

49. Alan Tracheberg, *Reading American Photographs: Images as History, Matthew Brady to Walker Evans*, New York, 1989, p.6, quoted in Lary May, 'Old Wine in New Bottles: Photography and the American Myth', *Reviews in American History*, Vol 19, No. 1 (March 1991) pp.54-59
50. Holmes and Wilson, 1994, p.84
51. Mansfield, quoted in Homes and Wilson, 1994, p.87
52. Holmes and Wilson, p.84
53. Photo caption, Holmes and Wilson, 1994, p.84
54. Photo caption, Holmes and Wilson, 1994, p.93
55. Roger Mansfield, 'The Source: a tale of the origins of British Surfing', *Wavelength*, 1994
56. For example, the 1976 *Blue Book Guide to Cornwall* carries a photo of Watergate Bay captioned 'This is the Malibu Beach' 1976, p.50.
57. For example, see 'Giant Waves Hit Cornwall', *The Sun*, 15 February 2006. 'WAVE goodbye to the Hawaiian surfing hotspot Waikiki. This is NEWQUAY'. ... Photographer Will Comer said: "It was breathtaking. Apart from the weather it could have been Hawaii." http://www.thesun.co.uk/sol/homepage/news/article37975.ece (accessed 19 February 2008)
58. Holmes and Wilson, 1994, pp.83-84
59. 'In 1963 there were about five people surfing but by 1965 we were our own little tribe, getting bigger all the time. By virtue of age I was on the outside but they very much embraced me even though they were grown men. I had quite a tribal upbringing.'. Roger Mansfield, '"I was a Tolcarne Gremmie" and other revelations from Britain's first surf rats' *The Surfer's Path*, 1(9), (1998), p.43.
60. Mansfield, 1994, p.24
61. Holmes and Wilson 1994, p.80
62. Chris Jones quoted in Holmes and Wilson (1994), 87. The surfer's name 'Mystic Rock' is undoubtedly a corruption of its original Cornish name Lystry, via the English 'mystery'. The significance of this rock in earlier times in reflected in the original Cornish name for Newquay, which before about 1600 was known as Tewyn P'lystry. Carter refers to 'ships rounding the Headland still ha[ving] to cross the rocky bight of Gazzle Bay and clear the inner spur off which lay the Old Dane and submerged Listrey rocks.' *Cornish Shipwrecks* Vol 2, The North Coast, 1970, p.121.
63. Holmes and Wilson, 1994, pp.80, 82, 89
64. Homes and Wilson, 1994, pp.84, 87
65. Pete Russell quoted in Holmes and Wilson, 1994,
66. Holmes and Wilson (1994), p.85
67. Holmes and Wilson (1994), p.89
68. Law, Lisa, Bunnell and Ong, 'The Beach, the gaze and film tourism' *Tourist Studies* (7)2, 2007, pp.141-164, 151; see also Baerenholdt, J., Haldrup, M., Larsen J., and Urry, J. *Performing Tourism Places*, London 2004
69. http://www.rogermansfield.com/cribbar.html accessed 19 February 2008
70. Fistral not safe', *Wavelength*, 31, February/March 1991, p.46
71. Letter 'Toxic Mutant Sewage Surfers' *Wavelength*, p.31, February/March 1991
72. Terrence Rafferty, 'The Monster That Morphed Into a Metaphor', *New York Times*, 2 May 2004, http://ccat.sas.upenn.edu/~haroldfs/popcult/handouts/metaphor/godzilla/godzilla.html (accessed 8 August .2008)
73. John Conway, quoted in Holmes and Wilson, 1994, p.83
74. Quoted in Matt Warshaw *The Encyclopaedia of Surfing*, 2003, 2005, p.649
75. *London Evening Standard*, 17.12.2004 http://www.thisislondon.co.uk/news/article-15399339-details/Monster+wave/article. (accessed 19 February 2008)
76. *Independent*, 18.02.2006 http://findarticles.com/p/articles/mi_qn4158/is_20060218/ai_n16151984 (accessed 20.02.08)
77. *Daily Mail* 9 January 2008 http://www.dailymail.co.uk/pages/live/articles/news/news.html?in_article_id=507033&in_page_id=1770 (accessed 19.02.2008)
78. *Western Morning News*, January 2006. source: http://reverttotype.blogspot.com/2006/06/newquays-giant-cribbar-wave.html#1 (accessed 24 June 2008)
79. Terrence Rafferty, *The Monster That Morphed Into a Metaphor*, New York Times, 2 May .2004, http://ccat.sas.upenn.edu/~haroldfs/popcult/handouts/metaphor/godzilla/godzilla.html (accessed 8 August 2008)
80. *Surfersvillage Global Surf News*, 1 February 2006, http://www.globalsurfnews.com/news.asp?Id_news=20145 (accessed 19 February 08)
81. *Western Mail* 28.01.06 http://icwales.icnetwork.co.uk/news/feature-news/tm_objectid=16638550&method=full&siteid=50082&headline=-i-conquered-a-real-sea-monster--name_page.html (accessed 19 February 2008)
82. *Daily Mail* 09 January 2008 http://www.dailymail.co.uk/pages/live/articles/news/news.html?in_article_id=507033&in_page_id=1770 Accessed 19.02.08
83. 'Surfers Ride Newquay's Giant Cribbar Wave', *Daily Telegraph*, 3 July .2008. http://www.telegraph.co.uk/news/uknews/2236574/surfers-ride-newquay's-giant-cribbar-wave accessed 5 July 2008.

See also 'Widow Maker alert…' on Roger Sharp's weblog at http://www.surfphoto.co.uk/ for 4 July 2008, which offers a useful, but relatively rare insider critical perspective to the media representation of Cribbar typified by the Telegraph article, by one of the UK's leading surf photographers. For example, on the photo caption accompanying the article, Sharp comments: ' "A local Newquay surfer rides the 25ft Cribbar..." rides is a pretty big generalisation for what is already obviously a pretty horrendous wipeout." '

84. See for example the surf reports and forecasts available on http://magicseaweed.com/Newquay-Fistral-Surf-Report/1/ and http://www.a1surf.com/surfcheck-fistralcam.html (accessed 5 November 2008)
85. Matt Warshaw, *The Encyclopaedia of Surfing*, (2005), pp.643-645
86. Googling 'big wave videos' produces over 59 million results. 'Cribbar videos' produces 3,600
87. John Conway, quoted in Holmes and Wilson (1994), pp.82-83
88. Riding Giants (2004) directed by Stacy Peralta was one of the few surf documentaries to have general cinema release in the UKC

Contributors

Graham Busby is an Associate Professor in Tourism Management with the School of Tourism and Hospitality at the University of Plymouth. He has lectured and published extensively on a broad range of topics relating to tourism including education, film, literature and church heritage.

Laura Cripps is Assistant Professor of Anthropology at Howard Community College in the USA. She played a leading role in the Cornish Audio Visual Archive's '21st Century Celts' conference in 2006. Her PhD research explored the spatial relationships of the late Iron Age and Early Roman settlement landscapes of Cornwall.

Monica Emerich is President of Groundwork Research & Communications in the USA. She is a noted author of books like *The Gospel of Sustainability: Media, Market and LOHAS* (2011) and her research focus is the cultural analysis of sustainability, as that concept is formed through media and the marketplace as a spiritualised lifestyle.

Melanie Giles is Lecturer in Archaeology at the School of Arts, Histories & Cultures at the University of Manchester. Her PhD studies at the University of Sheffield explored the Iron Age landscapes of East Yorkshire and current research interests focus on the late Bronze Age-late Iron Age archaeology of Britain, Ireland and north-west Europe.

Jesse Harasta is a doctoral candidate at Syracuse University in New York State in the USA and is currently writing a thesis about the social and political history of the Cornish Language Revival. He has been working on Cornish issues and travelling to Cornwall on fieldwork trips since 2006

Alan M. Kent is a Lecturer in Literature with the Open University in the South West of Britain and Visiting Lecturer in Celtic Studies at the University of La Coruña in Galicia. He is the author of numerous works and articles on the literary and cultural history of Cornwall and is also an acclaimed poet, novelist and dramatist.

Robert Keys is Director of Film Studies for the Cornish Audio Visual Archive. He has lectured in Cornish Studies, European History and Russian & Soviet Studies, with particular reference to film and folklore. His current research interests are the history of cinema in Cornwall and the historical analysis of Cornish Folktale collections.

Kay Milden is Project Manager for the 'Quarry Voices' oral history project based at Plymouth City Museum and an Honorary Research Fellow at the University of Exeter's History Department. Her PhD explored Cornish Methodism through oral history and she has published several articles relating to family and community studies.

Geoffrey Swallow's 2008 dissertation for the MA in Cornish Studies at the University of Exeter was the first extended academic treatment of the cultural history of surfing in Cornwall. He is currently researching the cultural construction of early sea bathing in West Cornwall and writing a book on annual swimming matches in Victorian Cornwall.

David Thomson is currently working for the Open University and was formerly at Truro College where he established its Foundation Degree in History, Heritage & Archaeology. He obtained his MPhil from the University of Exeter. Current interests include slavery and the abolition movements, as well as religious reforms in Early Modern England.

Garry Tregidga is Director of the Cornish Audio Visual Archive and Assistant Director of the Institute of Cornish Studies, University of Exeter. His research interests include oral history, cultural memory, and the political and spiritual identities of Cornwall and Celtic Britain since the late nineteenth century.